Sidcot Meeting House today

Quakers at Sidcot

1690-1990

Valerie Leimdorfer

Dear Friends, dwell in the everlasting seed of God,
in which you all will feel life eternal, that never hath an end.
And in that meet, and keep your Meetings.
And dwell together in the love and life of God,
with which you may all be filled.

George Fox, 1656

Published by Sidcot Preparative Meeting
1990

Published in 1990 by
Sidcot Preparative Meeting
Sidcot
Avon

Origination by
Ex Libris Press
1 The Shambles
Bradford on Avon
Wiltshire

Typeset in Plantin by Manuscript, Trowbridge

Printed in Great Britain by BPCC Wheatons Ltd., Exeter

ISBN 0 948578 98 X

© Valerie Leimdorfer

To Tom, with love

CONTENTS

Acknowledgements	9
Map	10
EARLY DAYS	13
Birth of a New Meeting	13
Organisation	13
Sufferings	15
MONTHLY MEETING	18
Marriages	19
Discipline	21
Collections and Distributions to the Poor	23
Meetings for Worship	24
Sidcot Particular Meeting	25
INTO THE EIGHTEENTH CENTURY	29
William Reeve Jnr.	29
William Jenkins and his School 1699-1728	31
POOR FRIENDS AT SIDCOT	35
William Watts	35
Sarah Beess	36
Mary Hucker	36
Gabriell Ballet	37
Jane Hardige	37
TRAVELLING FRIENDS	39
Including: Thomas Storey	39
Isaac Sharples	40
John Fothergill	40
Ruth Follows	40
John Churchman	40
Mary Dudley	40
Gossip	41
Preparative Meetings	43
The Hipsley Family	44
John Thomas	47
Martha Vowles and Charles Strode	49
John Benwell	50
The Sidcot Ghost	51
The Chest	52
Books	52
Money	53

THE NEW MEETING HOUSE 1817   57
    Weston-super-Mare Meeting House, and Fire Insurance   58
    The Fire of 1858   59
    The Seaman Family   60
    The Tanner Family   61
    More Deaths at Sidcot   63
    The Alterations to the Meeting House   64
    Other Meeting Houses   66
    New Boundaries   68
    Sidcot Preparative Meeting Minutes   68
    Charles Gilpin and William Tallack   70
    The Franco-Prussian War and other concerns   70
    The Care of the Meeting House   72
    Tirennial Reports on the Life of the Meeting   73

THIS CENTURY   75
    The Library   75
    Lectures   75
    The First World War   77
    The New School Hall   78
    REMINISCENCES   82
       Including Brief Individual Reminicences   82
       The Meeting House Gallery (1961)   90
       The North Wing (1984)   91
    Sewell House   93
    The School and the Meeting   95
    The Autumn Sale   97
    Other Fund Raising Activities   98
    Walks and Picnics   98
    The Sidcot Panel of the Quaker Tapestry   100
    Sidcot Meeting Now ... and then   101

Appendix I   Some Acts of Parliament under which Quakers suffered   107

Appendix II   The Eleven Particulars 1698 (much summarised)   109

Appendix III   Minutes of the Monthly Meeting at Woodborough the 1st of the 6th month 1701 (at William Reeve's)   110

Appendix IV	Quarterly Meeting Queries recommended by Yearly Meeting 1755	111
Appendix V	List of P.M. Clerks from 1847 and M.M. Clerks from 1873	113
Appendix VI	P.M. Accounts for the year 1988	115
List of Members	Explanatory Note	116
	Up to 1921	117
	From 1922 to 1989	147
Bibliography and References		159

ACKNOWLEDGEMENTS

When I embarked on this project over four years ago I had little idea what would be involved. I only knew that Tom King, a much respected member of our meeting, who had recently died, had the idea of writing a history for the tercentenary, and at the time no one else seemed concerned about the fact that the meeting would be 300 years old in 1990! I volunteered to do the research with the intention of producing just a booklet, but I was overwhelmed by information and I have ended up having to cut it down even for this book.

There are so many people to thank for their assistance, I do not know where to begin. Aubrey Hill offered his help in an unguarded moment and his hard work in compiling the list of members from 1922 onwards saved me a tremendous amount of time. Dick and Joyce Hinton not only gave me a great deal of support and encouragement, but compiled the material for the photographs, carefully reproduced by Bob Bowen. He and Desmond Simonds kindly took some pictures especially for this book. Frank Williams wrote several most useful notes which helped to spur me on. Amongst others who wrote letters or notes with helpful reminiscences are Kay Baker, David Birmingham, Bill Brown, John Crawley, Grace Freem, Ruth Fawell, Joan Hewitt, David Lindley, Olive and Wallace Litten, Margaret Lloyd, Arthur Marsden, Barabara Pask, Evelyn Phillips, Frances Reynolds, Peter Robson, Kenneth Southall, Margaret Stone, Grace Taplin and Joshua Watts. The staff of the Library at Friends House kindly photocopied several lists of members for me for the years from 1875-1921.

Marjorie Mallik conveyed me to the Taunton records office at a time when I was no longer very mobile, braving a horrendous traffic jam on the M5. Gill Bedingfield took me to Taunton before my illness took over and I thank her for that. Many other friends offered similar practical help and took me out for meals, drives and craft group meetings to provide a change of scenery and thus helped to keep my spirits up. Ted Milligan, Stephen Morland and Jean Plant read the early drafts and gave encouragement and helpful suggestions, while David and Valerie Major helped greatly with the final proof-reading. At the earliest stages, Philip Gale's work on the Sidcot archives, complete with meticulous notes, provided an ideal starting point. Most of all, my grateful thanks are due to my husband, Tom, who sat at 'Amy' (our word-processor) typing from dictation when I was too ill, taught me how to use 'Amy', and gave me support all the way through. Without him this book would not have been written.

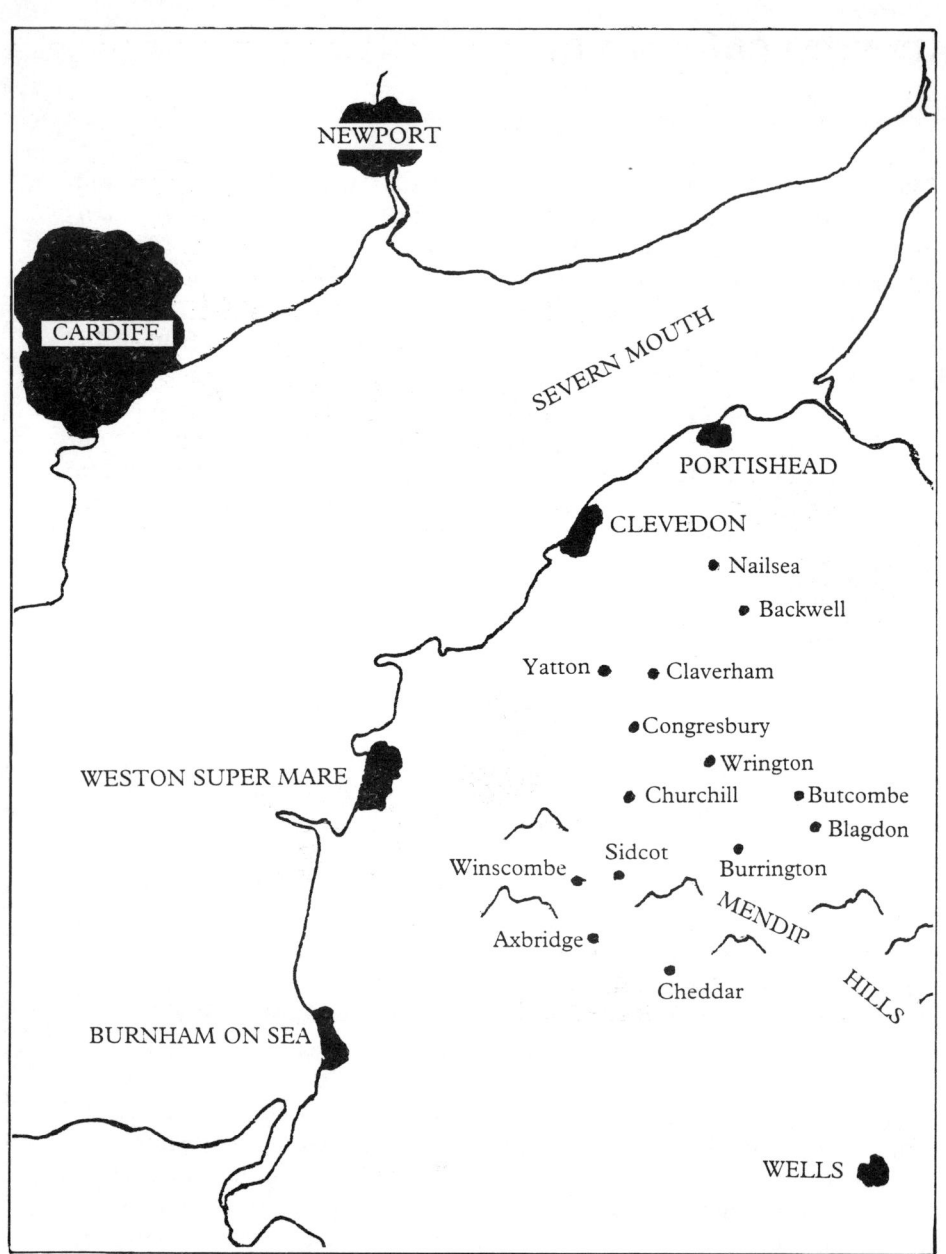

NOTE

It may be worthy of note, for the benefit of those whose memories do not stretch back more than two decades, that

£1 (100p) = 240d or 20 shillings
1s (5p) = 12d (old pence)

It will also help readers to note that the calendar was changed at the turn of the year 1751-52. After December 1751, January was called the 1st month, February the second month etc.. Previous to this, the year had started in March.

Throughout the book, in Friends' parlance, the First Day was Sunday, the Second Day was Monday etc.

EARLY DAYS

Birth of a new Meeting
On the 19th April 1690, Timothy Willis of Rowberrow bought the cottage and plot of ground at Harbury Batch, Sidcot, from Robert Stock for £25 for 1,000 years 'and every year one peppercorn being lawfully demanded'. The property was '60 ft length 30 ft breadth and bounded with the Kings Highway leading from Bristol to Axbridge on the North and West and the way that leadeth from Sidcott to Woodburrow on the South side'.. His attorneys were his 'trusty and well beloved friends', two local Quakers, John Dory of Butcombe and William Reeve the younger of Woodborough. On the following day, the 20th April 1690, he handed over the property to four trustees for 1000 years for 10 shillings and a yearly rent of one peppercorn 'to and for the use and behoof of the people of God now called Quakers by what name or names title or titles of Distinction soever they may hereafter be called'. The four trustees were William Lawrence of Axbridge, draper, John Lovell of Burrington, tanner, William Reeve jnr. of the parish of Winscombe, husbandman, and John Lovell jnr. of Churchill, also a tanner.

On the day before all this took place, at a Monthly Meeting held at Chew Magna on the 18th of the second month (April) 1690, 'Timothy Willis proposed his intention of Marryedge with Sarah Davis of Winscombe'. This must have been an exciting three days, not only for Timothy Willis but for other Friends in the district. At last, they would have an official Meeting House after the years when the threats of disturbance and persecution were ever present. There had been Meeting Houses established at Portishead (about 1670) and Claverham (1674), but until the Toleration Act of 1689, most meetings were held in private homes. Houses licensed in 1689 as Places of Worship included those of Thomas Smith at Cheddar, William Lawrence at Axbridge and John Gardner at Burrington. Sidcot Meeting was registered in 1690.

Organisation
The country had been in religious turmoil when George Fox set out to preach his message of spiritual honesty. He found there were people ready to listen to him and who had also found that 'there was one, even Christ Jesus' who could speak to their condition; that they did not need priests to tell them what they should believe, but personal experience of the light of Christ within. Others were willing and eager to spread the good news throughout the country. Quakerism reached North Somerset by way of Bristol in 1654. George Fox first passed

through Somerset on his return from Launceston prison in 1656. Jasper Batt of Street made a list of the 'First Publishers and Receivers of Truth' which was 'in and about the year 1656, and some time since'. Those included in the list were John Audland of Westmorland, and Thomas Briggs and John Braithwaite of Lancashire, who 'did publish trueth about the same time, in severall market townes, and had severall meetings in the same county (Somerset)..... And John Braithwaite, being a young man, there finished his testimony by death'. Thomas Salthouse of Lancashire, accompanied by Miles Halhead also had 'good service for the Lord there'. Jasper Batt who lists himself as 'being soone convict after their first coming, had a dispensation of the Gosple, committed to him' and several others of the county felt called to be ministers.

Among the first receivers were listed several near Sidcot. 'John Baker of Berrington freely received them and gave up his house for meetings for the Service of Trueth'. Henry Moore of Burnham and William Lawrence of Axbridge were also ready to entertain ministers at their homes and held meetings there.

In 1659, forty-five Friends met together at Glastonbury to consider 'advice and proposalls' for Friends in the area, including 'North and Northeast of Mendip'. It suggested among other things that someone from each meeting should keep a record of all sufferings, to be brought to the next General Meeting, and that a register should be kept of births, deaths and marriages in each meeting. There was also advice about ending disputes, bringing up children and caring for the poor. So by the time George Fox came again in 1668 on his travels through the county, to set up meetings 'about the supply of the poor and other affairs of the church', there was already some structure and it seems that the meeting with George Fox regularised this.

In each county a General Meeting of men Friends was to be held every quarter (soon to be called Quarterly Meeting) with men's Monthly Meetings in between for the different areas. George Fox 'came to Ilchester in Somersetshire, where we had a General Mens Meeting, and there settled the Monthly Meetings for that county in the Lord's everlasting power' (Fox's Journal 1668). The county was divided into three Monthly Meeting areas: Ilchester MM, West Somerset MM and the MM Beyond Mendip (or Northern MM). The places where meetings were to be kept in the MM area were listed as:

  Brislington and Keinsham
  Publoe
  Chew
  Hollotroe
  Bath and Bathford
  Froome
  Freshford
  Burton, Backwell & Naylsey

Porshutt (Portishead) & Walton
Berrington & Cheddar

A list of respected Friends was made who were considered 'meete to keep the mens meetings'. Seven friends are listed by name for Burrington and Cheddar: John Dory, John Baker, Timothy Willis, Thomas Smith, Richard Yeepe, William Lawrence, and William Lovell.

Sufferings
It was not surprising that when the early Quakers preached against the "vain customs" of the world, the world would not take it lightly. Nor is it surprising that when they stood in the parish church, which they called a 'steeplehouse', and denounced the 'world's worship', the priests did not accept it. Although their message was what many people had been waiting for, the more who were convinced, the more those who felt threatened tried to stop them.

The early Quakers were strong and immutable in their beliefs. They refused to pay tithes, or rates to the Church of England, for the upkeep of churches and the payment of ministers, and to make use of any minister for marriage or burial or any other cause. They refused to swear an oath, considering the words of Jesus 'swear not at all' (Matt. 5.34) to be a positive command which should not be broken and on the principle that truth should always be spoken. They met publicly for worship in silent waiting upon the spirit of God, they spoke out against vice and immorality in market places and fairs, they refused to take their hats off or bow to anyone no matter how important their position, used the same language to all, rich or poor, and refused to fight or bear arms or to hire others to do so instead.

Under Oliver Cromwell's Commonwealth there were no specific laws made against Quakers. In fact, his government accepted liberty of conscience, and Oliver Cromwell himself made fine speeches on the subject. But in spite of the good words, he was not able to stop local magistrates from passing harsh sentences on Quakers. There were plenty of old laws which could be used against them (see Appendix I) and if accusations, such as disturbing the peace, refusing to pay tithes, or contempt of court were not enough to convict them, they could always be required to swear on oath. They refused to pay fines, saying that they were not guilty in the sight of God, and so usually ended up in prison. Over 200 were imprisoned in Ilchester gaol between December 1660 and March 1661. Many were soon released, but Ilchester prison was the centre of organisation for Somerset Quakerism for many years.

Joseph Besse lists in all about 850 who suffered in some way before 1689. After the Toleration Act priests could still demand tithes, and they did. A book which was 'Humbly submitted to the Consideration of the MEMBERS of both HOUSES of PARLIAMENT' lists 107 prosecutions in Somerset between the years 1696 and 1736. Thirty of those prosecuted were imprisoned and one died in prison. This was second only to the number prosecuted in Yorkshire.

John Whiting, a Friend from Nailsea who later moved to Wrington and started a meeting there wrote a book about his life, entitled "Persecution Exposed". According to him, Quarterly Meeting was usually held in the hall of the Friary at Ilchester, which was then part of the prison. In September 1680 Justice Walrond came with a troop of horsemen to prevent the meeting by locking the doors so that visiting Friends could not get in, nor prisoners out. The Quarterly Meeting on that occasion was held at the local inn where the landlord was 'no Friend, but a friendly man'. The landlord was fined £60 (£20 each for the Quarterly Meetings of men and women held in separate rooms, and another £20 for appealing to Quarter Sessions), but Friends reimbursed him. Amongst those present (who were also fined 5s each for attending) were John Dory, John Lovell, John Baker, John Plumley and William Reeve from the Burrington and Cheddar area. There were altogether 44 men and 27 women present even though the Friends in prison were prevented from joining the meeting.

The severity of the imprisonment varied, depending mainly on the attitude of the jailer, but John Whiting was able to make several visits to Bristol during the period of his imprisonment. However, after the Monmouth rebellion in 1685, he was handbolted to John Hipsley from Chew for five weeks and three days "till the wrists of John Whiting had the skin worn off by means of the Irons". When people refused to pay tithes, the common practice was to take goods from them worth the equivalent, or more, but priests could also have recourse to law, either in the bishop's court or the civil court. Some priests reacted violently to Quakers, especially after the restoration of Charles II in 1660, when the power of the Church of England was re-established.

How did the Quakers near Sidcot fare? John Baker of Burrington, who was one of the first 'receivers of truth' in Somerset was also one of the first in the area to suffer. He had goods worth £2 10s taken for tithes in 1658. In the same year, Edith Mitchell, also of Burrington, was committed to prison for eight weeks 'for speaking to the Priest and people there'. The Justice Cole who sent her there was 'so virulent against the Quakers, that when a sheep-stealer was brought before him, he spake to him thus: "I will send you to Gaol to the Quakers, and you shall go to the Gallows together"'. Joseph Besse (the chronicler of Sufferings) notes that Justice Cole did not live long after this, but was taken ill suddenly as he was about to set out on a journey, and died the same day.

In 1662 Thomas Smith of Cheddar had a cow taken worth £3 10s. Later, in 1681, 'William Goodridge had taken from him on an execution for tithes cattle worth £50'. He came from Banwell, and spent some time in prison, as did Samuel Sayer, who eventually died there in 1682, having been a prisoner for more than six years. James Plumly, George Plumly, John Young and John Plumly, labourers of Priddy, had goods taken in 1670. They were fined 3s each for not appearing at public worship. When the bailiffs came they took an overcoat worth 8s from James Plumly, three pewter plates worth 12s from George Plumly, and a pot worth 14s from John Young. When John Plumly refused to pay, the officers realised that they had taken goods from him four years previously which had been sold. There was still 4s of that money left so they kept the 3s and offered him the one shilling back. When he refused, they threw it on the ground and rode away, but a neighbour found the coin and gave it to a poor child in the same parish.

John Dory of Butcombe had goods taken on three occasions for absence from public worship, on the second occasion in 1679 George Pearce of Winscombe and Timothy Willis of Rowberrow also had goods taken. In 1682, William Lawrence, a tailor from Axbridge, who was also one of the first 'receivers of truth' in Somerset, was cited at Wells for absence from public worship. Joseph Besse gives an account of the conference between William Lawrence and the Archdeacon, who became enraged by the comments of the former relating to the ignorance of those who had been educated at Oxford. William Lawrence was dragged to the house of the Bishop's Chancellor where he was abused and tendered the Oath of Allegiance. He refused to swear, and was committed to prison for nine months.

John Watts of Nepnett had 81 horseloads of wheat, value £6, taken from him in 1683. This was twice as much as the priest, Charles Simms, could lawfully claim. The same priest also took 90 sheaves of wheat from Robert Line, 'the Priest himself throwing down some with his own Hands'. This same Robert Line of Burrington had been in trouble with Friends, as minuted in the General meeting minutes 24th of seventh month (September) 1668: 'having been visited by Friends in love', he had been offensive towards them. Friends, including John Baker and John Dory, were again appointed to visit him to try to convince him 'of the evil of his ways'. Clearly, they were successful if he not only remained with Friends but was prepared to suffer for his convictions. John Dory also had sacks of wheat 'pulled down by the servants of Arthur Hearn, Priest of Blagdon, who carried them away in what quantities they pleased'.

About this time, Justices disturbed a meeting at Claverham and ordered Friends to depart and when they refused, their names were taken. Afterwards, warrants were issued by which goods were taken from those who had been present. The goods included several cows which local people refused to buy, and which the Justice had to take into his own custody until they were sold to his brother-in-law. A meeting at the home of Daniell Holbrook of Chew was violently broken into by John Helliar, Under Sherriff for the County, and several bailiffs. John Helliar ordered them to search John Hipsley for arms saying, "He looks like a Rogue", and using other abusive language. He then ordered the bailiffs to secure the Friends while he went to dinner with Doctor Cross, the parson. He returned two hours later, bringing some of the parson's faggots with him and threatened to set the house on fire, much to the consternation of the neighbours. In the end, they threw out the benches and burned them. John

Hipsley and another Friend were dragged by the hair, Joseph Taylor was struck with an axe and over 40 Quakers were arrested and accused of 'riotously, routously, seditiously, tumultously and unlawfully' assembling together 'to disturb the peace of our Lord the King'. They were, of course, sitting in silence.

Another story, which illustrates the way the neighbours felt and the influence which could be brought to bear on the persecutors, at least according to Joseph Besse (an 18th century writer), is the story of Thomas Smith of Cheddar. Twenty years on from the time he had one cow taken, he suffered a much worse fate. In 1682, 'on the 11th of the Month called April this Year, two Bailiffs came to the House of Thomas Smith, of Cheddo, an ancient Yeoman of good Repute, who had been prosecuted for Tithes, at the Suit of George Doddington Esq.; to a Sequestration; they entered the House, and seized all his Goods, shutting him and his Family out of Doors, telling him that He must go and agree with Esquire Doddington. The honest Man, knowing that in this Case he could not consent to pay any Thing, procured another Dwelling for himself and Family, bore the Loss of his Goods with the Meekness and Patience of a true Christian sufferer. His Neighbours began to reflect on the Persons who had thus turned an innocent Man and his Family out of Doors, and those Reflections came to the Hearing of the Esquire, in whose Name the Suit had been carried on; He considering the Man's Case, to clear himself of the popular Imputation of Cruelty on this Occasion, generously sent back the Key of the House by his Servant to the said Thomas Smith, and restored to him the Possession of all his Goods; his peaceable and quiet Demeanour, under his Sufferings, having an effectual Reach upon the Prosecutor, and moving him to commiserate the Case of Man who gave so convincing a Proof of his being really conscientious'.

MONTHLY MEETING

The men's Monthly Meeting in North Somerset kept minutes from 1667, the year before George Fox visited Ilchester, and Monthly Meetings were formally set up. Meetings were held in the houses of Friends and were usually well attended. Friends from local meetings attended Monthly Meeting and sometimes had to travel a long way. Representatives were appointed to record the relevant information and report it to Quarterly Meeting, which meant more travelling.

While it was usually the same people who attended Monthly Meeting, apart from those listed as being present there were always people coming and going, proposing intentions of marriage, justifying their alleged misdeeds etc.. The business covered by Monthly Meeting included marriages, finance and relief of poor Friends, apprenticeships, and discipline including testimonies against Friends. There is little mention in the early minutes of sufferings or of meetings for worship, or of meeting houses. The minutes for third month (May 1690) contain no reference to the acquisition of Sidcot Meeting House.

No records survive of the early women's Monthly Meeting, but it is men-

EARLY DAYS

tioned in the men's minutes for 1675, and in 1695 John Whiting proposed 'the reviving of a Women's Meeting on the side of Clavum', i.e. Sidcot, Claverham and Portishead. The women agreed, and their first meeting was held at Sidcot on the 20th of fifth month (July) 1696. In fifth month 1697 they took over the distribution of money to the poor; forty shillings was given to them and they were to give an account once a quarter. John Whiting was to give them a list of poor Friends from the minute book. They continued to give relief to the poor until the end of 1699, when 'for som reasons' they gave it up to the men again. The 'reasons' may have had something to do with the fact that Sarah and John Whiting had moved to London that year.

Marriages

In 1659, at a meeting in Glastonbury, Somerset Quakers laid down the formalities for marriage, and it was an important function of Monthly Meetings (and Quarterly Meetings until 1684) to see that the correct procedure was followed. The early proposals were modified several times, but the duties of the Monthly Meeting remained much the same. These included ensuring that both the parties consented, that they were both clear of other ties, that parents gave their consent, that proper provision was made for children of a previous marriage and that they were both good Quakers. They were not allowed to marry someone who was not a Quaker nor to marry a relative as near as a second cousin, so choice was rather limited. Although in a testimony against Friends' children 'marrying out', young men are reproved for looking 'into the world for wives instead of ... looking among Friends, where they might find such as are tenfold more worthy ...' and young women are described as tempted 'to be drawn aside by some that do not compare perhaps to what they might have had, even in the outward', if they had looked amongst Friends.

Two or three Friends were appointed by Monthly Meeting to look into the 'clearness' of the people who announced their intention of marriage. This gives an idea of where the various Friends came from, as usually the minutes give an indication of the place of residence of the couple and those who were chosen to make enquiries usually came from the same district. When a couple had given notice of intention of marriage, their engagement was binding.

When a couple's marriage was not allowed, or when they realised it would not be allowed, they sometimes carried on regardless and had a 'disorderly marriage'. The first such disorderly marriage at Sidcot was of one Martin Saunders of Banwell (who was often in trouble with Friends) who in 1692 'came to a meeting of Friends at Sidcott and presumptuously declared himselfe to take a woman viz. Sarah Saunders by name, to be his wife, out of the profession of the Truth, and contrary to the advice of Friends'. He was disowned, but seems to have taken no notice and continued to cause trouble, so he was disowned again in 1704.

Not only Sidcot Friends had disorderly marriages in Sidcot Meeting. John

Whereas Wm Herbert of Wey[...] in the County of [...] Distiller, Son of Wm Herbert of East Cowes In the Isle of Wight and County of Southton, Mariner, and Mary Davis of Axbridge In ye County of Somerset, Spinster, Daughter of Gabriel Davis of Yeaton, in ye County aforesaid, Deceased

Having Declared their Intentions of taking each other in Marriage before several Publick Meetings of the People of God called Quakers in ye Countys of Dorset and Somerset, according to the Good Order used among them, whose Proceedings therein, after a deliberate Consideration thereof (with regard unto the Righteous Law of God, and Example of his People Recorded in the Scriptures of Truth in that Case) were Approved by the said Meetings, they appearing Clear of all others, and having Consent of Parties and Relations Concerned.

Now these are to Certifie All whom it may Concern, That for the full accomplishing of their said Intentions, this fifth day of the fifth Month, called July in the Year, according to the English Account, One Thousand Seven Hundred & Seven. They the said Wm Herbert and Mary Davis appeared in a Publick Assembly of the aforesaid People, and others met together for that Purpose in their Publick Meeting-Place at Sidcott in ye County of Somerset aforesaid in a Solemn Manner, he the said Wm Herbert taking the said Mary Davis by the Hand, did openly declare as followeth, Friends in the Fear of the Lord, and in the Presence of this Assembly, I take this my Friend Mary Davis, to be my Wife, promising through the Lords Assistance, to be unto Her a Loving and faithfull Husband, untill by Death, we shall be Seperated.

And then and there in the said Assembly, the said Mary Davis did in like manner declare as followeth, Friends in ye Fear of the Lord, and in the Presence of this Assembly I take this my Friend Wm Herbert, to be my Husband, promising through the Lords Assistance to be unto him, a Loving and faithfull Wife, untill by Death, we shall be Seperated (or words to that purpose)

And the said William and Mary as a further Confirmation thereof, did then and there to these Presents set their Hands. And we, whose Names are hereunto Subscribed, being present among others, at the Solemnizing of their said Marriage and Subscription in manner aforesaid, as Witnesses hereunto, have also to these Presents Subscribed our Names, the Day and Year above written.

Marriage certificate of Mary Davis and William Herbert

EARLY DAYS

Hellier of Mark, who had already been in trouble in 1686 for taking up 'Armes in the late Insurrection' (i.e. the Monmouth rebellion), and was 'often found to break his promises in payment of money', came to Sidcot Meeting 'where unto he did not belong' and took a woman to be his wife without going through any of the preliminaries required. He was disowned at Quarterly Meeting on the 20th December 1694. Others went to a priest to be married and were disowned for this, unless they publicly condemned their own wickedness. It is worth noting here that in the eyes of the world, till Hardwicke's Marriage Act of 1753, marriages did not have to have a religious ceremony, and could be contracted privately by the consent of both parties. Quakers had very strict views, and if a couple were living together as man and wife, they were testified against, but some were allowed to marry later.

An early marriage certificate which has come to light is that of Mary Davis. She was married to William Herbert 'this fifth day of the fifth Month called July ...' 1711 (Old Calendar). He was a distiller from Weymouth, she was a spinster from Axbridge, the daughter of Gabriel Davis of Yatton. They appeared in the 'Meeting Place at Sidcott in the County of Somerset and in a Solemn Manner, he the said Wm. Herbert taking the said Mary Davis by the Hand, did openly declare as followeth, Friends in the Fear of the Lord, and in the Presence of this Assembly, I take this my Friend Mary Davis to be my Wife, promising through the Lord's Assistance to be unto Her a Loving and faithfull Husband , untill by Death we shall be Seperated'. She then said something similar and then they signed the certificate along with all those present. Mary Davis was engaged previously to a Samuel Chivers of Wydcombe, but Samuel died in 1709, before the wedding could take place. I hope she lived happily the second time.

Discipline

It was very hard to be a Quaker. As we have seen, many suffered imprisonment and torture or even death for their views. On the other hand, those who were not willing to undergo this suffering were testified against and disowned by the Society. There was to be no compromise of the Truth. In addition to this, Quakers were separated from society by the way they dressed and spoke. They did so as an attempt to break down the barriers between masters and servants, rich and poor, in what was an extravagant age, but eventually the externals of forms of speech and dress became seemingly more important than the basic message. In the first month (March) 1698, Quarterly Meeting drew up eleven particulars (Appendix II) which were circulated to Monthly Meetings and thence to each local meeting, which was then expected to send in reports on how their meeting was faring in respect of observing these requirements.

If Quakers misbehaved in any way, they were said to be 'disorderly walkers' and Monthly Meeting or Quarterly Meeting would appoint two or more Friends to visit them. These Friends would try to persuade them to mend their ways, and the visits were carried on as long as there was any hope of success. There is no doubt as to the patience and love in which most of these visits were carried out. Often the miscreant was asked to sign a paper condemning his or her sin and to read it in public or fix it in a public place. If the erring Quaker was still stubborn, as a last resort, a 'testimony' was drawn up against him or her and presented to the person concerned and also read out in the meeting he or she attended. The testimony always hoped for repentance, but disowned the evil-doer until that repentance was evident. Although this system seems cruel now, it stemmed from a loving desire that the miscreant would repent and that his or her soul should be saved. It was believed that 'departure from Truth' meant damnation of the soul. Sometimes it is fairly obvious from the testimony what the misdeed was, such as marriage by a priest, debt, or habitual drunkenness etc.. However, although the testimony was always very wordy, sometimes it hid the crime in very vague terms.

Sidcot Friends who were troublesome included the already mentioned Martin Saunders of Banwell, who as well as a disorderly marriage, was guilty amongst other things of 'fetching things with his plough for the casting of a bell'. Moreover, he tried to justify himself by saying he saw no evil in it 'only that he thought Friends would take occasion against him'. Friends found him 'very dark in his understanding'!

In 1694, Friends testified against living together before marriage in general, but in particular they 'expected that Henry Stone comply with this advice'. Henry Stone was from Banwell and appeared at Monthly Meeting saying that 'he had putt the young woman from him that lived in his house as a servant with him'. Two Friends were appointed to speak to the young woman, who had 'but little sense of Truth, but lately come amongst Friends'. Henry Stone obviously preferred not await Friends judgement on the matter, and three months later 'contrary to the good advice given him' took the woman to be his wife in Sidcot Meeting. A testimony was immediately drawn up against him.

Henry Stone had regularly received money from Friends when they distributed to the poor, so it must have been a sacrifice to have married like this. However, it seems that eventually Friends agreed that he made the right choice of wife. In 1711, he was again on the list, and he received regularly after that. When he died in 1719, his wife Elizabeth continued to receive money regularly.

The testimony in 1699 against 'the Degeneracy & outgoing of Many Friends' Children by forsaking Truth and marrying by Priest & such Parents as Connive at it or encourage itt' was in part occasioned by John Farmer of Sidcot Meeting who was having trouble with his daughters. Parents were advised to restrict the money in their childrens hands 'as have often been said, if they cannot rule their hearts, they might rule their purses'. Parents were also advised to use their utmost endeavours to keep them coming to meetings. John Farmer and his wife obviously succeeded with at least two of their children as Joseph Farmer married Sarah Board of Winscombe in Sidcot Meeting in 1706, and Judith Farmer and Thomas Adams were also married in Sidcot Meeting in 1708.

Collections and distribution to the poor

Collections were made when necessary for the Public Stock, which was a Quarterly Meeting fund, but collected and distributed by the Monthly Meetings. The first record of a collection is in 1682, when John Baker took in the contribution from Burrington and Cheddar which amounted to £3 17s 6d, which was the most (by 18s) of all meetings listed. In 1692 a collection was recommended by London Friends and Quarterly Meeting for distressed Friends in Ireland 'who have sustained greate losses by the late wars and distructions in that Kingdome. The severall collections of the meetings belonging to this Monthly Meeting are as followeth ... '

from	£	s	d
Frome	3	16	6
Hallitrow	2	11	6
Brislington & Cainsham	2	15	0
Portishead	4	2	6
Sidcot	8	18	6
Clarum	8	13	6
Bath Ford	1	6	3
Chew	6	18	0
Pensford	1	16	6
Total	£40	18	3

The total of £113 19s 0d received by Quarterly Meeting was so impressive that the contribution from each meeting was recorded in the minutes 'that so the charity of Friends may remaine as a good example in the future'. Street Meeting contributed £10, but apart from that Sidcot was top of the list, showing that it was the largest, most wealthy, or most generous meeting in the Monthly Meeting area. This was borne out by succeeding collections for the Public Stock, but around 1710 Sidcot was overtaken by Claverham.

Money collected was handed to a Receiver, who was responsible for payment, and occasionally gave accounts. It was agreed at Monthly Meeting at the end of 1687 that the Friend who kept the Public Stock should also keep a trunk, or box, where the 'writings' of meeting houses, burial grounds etc. were kept. John Dory of Butcombe was one of the first Receivers. Poor Friends were supported from the Public Stock, and payments were made by whichever member present at Monthly Meeting could most conveniently deliver it. This gives an indication as to where the poor people lived. One of the first mentioned in the Monthly Meeting minutes was Richard Stile of Burrington, when in 1667 William Lawrence was given 20s to 'supply his necessity'. Richard Stile died in 1668 and John Baker, John Dory, Timothy Willis and William Lawrence were 'to speake with the woman where he lay sicke and to discharge the coste'. From 1697 to 1699 the Women's Meeting dealt with the distribution of relief. Help was refused when a person was not accepted as a Quaker and some applicants were advised to apply to the parish for support.

Friends also left legacies to the poor. In 1686 Mary Baker, wife of John, left 20s to be disposed of by Friends 'to such poor Friends as they should thinke fitt'. William Lawrence and Timothy Willis also left legacies to be distributed to poor Friends.

The Public Stock could also be used for books, and carriage for books. In the 3rd month (May) 1681, it was agreed to pay William Lawrence 'for Books unsouled' £1 6s 6d. In 1692 'paid to Wm. Lawrence for carriage of 4 of G.F.s Journals & 2 of Wm. Penns Prefaces gave to Clareham, Sidcott, Portishead & Chew Meetings £0 4s 0d'. William Lawrence was to look after the one for Sidcot, which was for Friends 'use and service from tyme to tyme'.

Meetings for Worship

Meetings for worship were held regularly on first days, but on other days of the week as well, and both men and women attended these, although they usually sat on different sides of the room. Monthly Meetings for worship were also held in various places and visitors and Travelling Friends often turned up at these, so attempts were made to ensure that there were no clashes between such meetings. Again Friends had to travel fair distances across the country, but at the same time it was a way of catching up with the news.

The weekday meetings were seldom well attended, and throughout the two centuries when they were held, Friends were often exhorted to attend. The first of many exhortations that includes Sidcot was in the 10th month (December) 1691, as a postcript to Monthly Meeting minutes:

> Wee doe ... exhort and beseech all as they tender the good of theyer owne souls, to be dilligent in the wholesome and commendable practice of meeting togeather to waite upon God in theyer weakeday meetings as well as on first days, especially wee recommend revivall of some meetings which to our griefe wee understand are on the weake days, either totally neglected, or on greate measure declyned, in particular at Portishead, Clarum, Cainsham, Brislington & Sidcott, we desyre all concerned to search and examine the cause of this decay and coldness, and consider whether it may not be said to such as it was to some of old in another cause, If you love them that love you what thanks have ye, doe not sinners doe the same? Accordingly if we meet togeather to worship God only when we have another businesse, or are not allowed to minde our worldly concerns what reward have we? doe not even the professor and prophane doe soe likewise? Therefore Friends for the Lord's sake lett this be mended ... And the Lord quicken, strengthen and encouredge all in theyer duty herein... Subscribed in the behalfe of our

Monthly Meeting this 4th day of the 10th mo. 1691 by

John Hipsley	John Whiting	John Dando
Joseph Taylor	Richd. Vickris	Richd Amesbury
John Lovell	John Cowling	John Heale
Richard Thomas		

In 1698 Sidcot decided that their weekday meeting might be better attended if the day on which it was held was changed from a fourth to a fifth day. It was considered that it would be of benefit to travelling Friends. At the meeting when this was proposed, there was also a minute relating to the setting up of school. The change in day was to cause trouble later for William Jenkins, that school's first Master. However, for the time being the decision was recorded as follows:-

Att our Monthly Meeting at Belluton the 29th of the 5th month 1698...

As to the changing the weekly meeting day at Sitcutt from the 4th to 5th day, Wm Reeve gives an account that Friends of their meeting are willing, & do consent thereto. Therefore itt is ordered that it be held on the 5th day of the weeke for time to come & also that everey second 5th day of the month be held as a monthly meeting & that the 4th day before the said monthly meeting at Sidcutt, there be no weekly meeting at Claverham, nor no weekly meeting at Sitcutt the 5th day after the monthly meeting at Claverham, unless such as are not able to go, that Friends of both meetings may the better attend both those monthly meetings when they come, which was and is established for the services of truth, & therefore all Friends are desired to be dilligent therein for the honour of God, & good of their own soules.

Friends concern for simplicity did not seem to extend to the writing of minutes!

Sidcot Particular Meeting
A congregation that met periodically for worship was called a particular meeting and, unlike in business meetings, the men and the women sat together. In 1690 Sidcot Meeting must have been made up of Friends from Burrington and Cheddar Meetings and the original membership may have been something like this:

Axbridge	Edith Lawrence, Sarah Lawrence, William Lawrence, Walter Lawrence, Elizabeth Stoudly, Richard Stoudly
Banwell	Susan Austin, Edmund and Mary Jennings, Martin Saunders, Henry Stone

QUAKERS AT SIDCOT

Burrington	Sarah Beess, John jnr. and Mary Lovell, James Phelps, John Gardner
Butcombe	John and Frances Dory, Hannah Tucker
Charterhouse	Ezekiel Brock
Cheddar	Thomas Smith and family, Richard Yeepe & Richard Yeepe jnr.
Churchill	Mary Hippisley, William Parsons
Compton Bishop	Francis and Hannah Palmer
Havyat (Wrington)	William and Mary Lovell and their son John Lovell
Langford	John and Mary Lovell
Nepnett	Robert Lyne, John Watts and family, Rebecca and William Watts
Priddy	Ann and James Plumley, John Plumley Jane Plumley
Rowberrow	Joan Davis, Timothy Willis
Sidcot	William Croy, Sarah Davis
Shipham	John Farmer and family
Stock	Richard Hipsley
Westbury-sub-Mendip	Robert Holder
West Hay (Wrington)	Richard Plumley
Winscombe	Mary Tugwell, George Pearce
Winthill (Banwell)	Margaret and William Goodridge, Abraham Thomas
Woodborough	Thomas Reeve, Sarah and William Reeve, Mary and William Reeve jnr.

Above: *Old Meeting House and Cottage*
Below: *The Old Meeting House (Harbury Batch) today; its garden was the old Burial Ground*

QUAKERS AT SIDCOT

Worle   John Hucker and Mary Whiting
                                 Edmund Chappell (Jnr.), John Chappell

Of these, John Dory (d. 1696), William Lawrence (d. 1697), William Lovell, Thomas Smith (d. 1692), Timothy Willis (d. 1698), and Richard Yeep (d. 1693) were 'judged meete to keep the mens meetings' in 1668, but by 1690 they were getting old and by the end of the century, all except William Lovell had died. Nevertheless, there were several young men who were able to carry the meeting into the eighteenth century. Amongst these were Richard Hipsley, William Reeve jnr. and Abraham Thomas. Abraham Thomas was the son of Arthur Thomas (previously known as Arthur Brooks) of Cleeve, who was a very active early Friend and was amongst those 'judged meete to keep the mens meetings' in 1668 for Burton, Backwell and Nailsea. All three had seen the zeal with which the early Quakers wished to change the world and the suffering and love with which they went about trying to do so, but by 1700 attitudes were changing. Quakers were beginning to look in on themselves, to think of themselves as a race apart and to withdraw from the world. The age of 'Quietism' was beginning, and numbers began to decline. Nevertheless, while there were friends of such religious devotion, moral integrity and organisational ability, the Quakers of Sidcot were ready for the future.

INTO THE EIGHTEENTH CENTURY

William Reeve Jnr.
William Reeve, described as a husbandman or yeoman, lived on Woodborough Green about half a mile from Harbury Batch. His name appears on both the original deeds relating to the purchase and handing over of the cottage to be a meeting house, and he was one of the two Quakers who were described as 'trusty and well beloved Friends' by Timothy Willis. In fact, William was married in 1688 to Mary Willis, niece of Timothy Willis, who was living with her uncle in Rowberrow since her father had died. In the minutes of Monthly Meeting at Brislington for the 24th of 12th month 1687/8 (Feb. 1688) it is recorded that 'William Reeve appeared againe at this meeting with his Friend Mary Willis.... and John Doree gives an account to the meeting of the consent of the father and mother of the said William, and likewise of Timothy Willis, uncle of the said Mary....'

William Reeve had been amongst those who in September 1680 were prevented from meeting inside the prison at Ilchester. He was regular both at Quarterly Meeting and Monthly Meeting and the latter was often held at his house. Appendix III gives an example of the minutes of one such meeting.

William Reeve was concerned with collecting and returning the sufferings of Friends on account of tithes for Sidcot Meeting, which had to be done before every Quarterly Meeting. He also distributed money from the Public Stock to the poor, for example, to Henry Stone of Banwell. He also visited Henry Stone in order to warn him about living together with a woman before marriage, and to read the testimony against him afterwards. He usually took the collection for Sidcot Meeting, and was handed legacies and received loans. Many times he was appointed to visit someone, with some other Friend, to enquire about clearness for marriage, or to discuss some problem such as in the case of John Farmer's daughters. When Edmund Chappell's children were disobedient, he was called upon to advise him about the settlement of his estate. When the servant of John Lovell jnr. was living with him even though she was married to someone else, it was William Reeve who was to see her removed. We read in the minutes 'Wm. Reeve gives this meeting account that Sarah Sturdges is removed from John Lovell and hee signified to Wm. Reeve that hee was glad she is gon'.

In 1703 some Friends of Sidcot Meeting had been paying tithes. William Reeve and William Lovell had discussed it with them but, having failed to convince them, they were 'desired to take with them some more friends of theire meeting and if they cannott prevaill with them, then they are to desire them to come to our next meeting'. It was not until 1705 that the recalcitrant Friends actually turned up at Monthly Meeting.

Meanwhile, in 1704 there was a renewed testimony against Martin Saunders (whose wife had presumably died) who had been causing trouble again Although he had been disowned, he continued to attend meetings for worship. 'Now because this man hath ... come... to our meetings lest any that dont know thereof should count him one of us and so speak evil of our Profession for this mans sake, we found a concern upon us, considering his late wicked and scandelous conversation being accused (& we believe justly too) of being too familiar with his maid or woman servant, after wt manner we need not mention....'. He was desired to stay away from meetings until he showed signs of repentance. There followed a long sermon on repentance from Biblical texts, signed by all seventeen members present at Monthly Meeting. There were several testimonies drawn up against Friends of Sidcot Meeting and William Reeve had a hand in writing them, and presumably copying them. In 1702 he was paid '8s 6d for books at Q.M. and copying out an epistle'. In the same year, he and Abraham Thomas allowed their names to go forward as representatives for the next Yearly Meeting.

In 1704 orders were taken for George Fox's doctrinal books (price about 14s) at Sidcot. William Reeve, William Jenkins, William Lovell all ordered one. William Jenkins was the first schoolmaster and William Reeve was present at the Quarterly Meeting at Taunton where in the 4th month (June) 1699 his appointment was approved. One Joseph Hyde had previously offered his services as schoolmaster but 'Friends on enquiery doe thinck fitt to wave making use of him and William Reeve is appointed to write to him and give him an answer accordingly'.

When William Reeve died in 1707 he left £10 to be given to poor Friends in the county of Somerset, £2 of which were to be given to William Watts of Nepnett and £1 to John Hucker of Worle. Why William Watts was singled out for so much we shall never know but the legacy (which was not distributed till 1709) must have been a godsend as only in the previous month 'report was made to this meeting that Wm. Wats have had a fall from a horse and broke his arm hee being a poor helpless man Friends have sent him by John Hipsley 10s to releive him in his weak condition'. Perhaps he was an old friend of the family. William Watts appears in Quarterly Meeting minutes as early as 1668 being warned by Friends to 'beware the spiritt of the world which draws from truth'. He obviously heeded the warning and Friends looked after him and his wife Rebecca in their old age.

The picture we have of William Reeve is of a conscientious, trustworthy, busy man whose life was bound up with the Quakers. He travelled extensively around the area to Quarterly Meetings, Monthly Meetings, midweek meetings and also on many visits to Friends, for one reason or another, so he must have been a familiar figure on horseback riding around the neighbourhood. He clearly was able to work well with others, as there is nothing to indicate that there was any dispute, but when Sidcot Friends were having trouble with Ann Reeve (his sister-in-law), he was never appointed to visit and kept well away. He was mainly accompanied on his visits by Richard Hipsley, Abraham Thomas, William Lovell or William Jenkins. The latter seems to have been a different character.

William Jenkins and His School 1699-1728

There is no doubt that the presence of the school at Sidcot has kept the meeting alive. If Quarterly Meeting in December 1698 had decided on Long Sutton as the site for the proposed school, Sidcot Meeting would probably have disappeared along with Chew, Belluton and eventually Claverham. But there was an objection from the north division of the county 'doubting how the place proposed might agree with their children's health' and thus Sidcot was chosen. On the 22nd of the 4th month (June) 1699, at Quarterly Meeting at Taunton, William Jenkins of Hertford was appointed for two years in the first instance.

> From the 1st of 6th month next viz:
> for teaching Greek, Latin, writing & Arithmetick after the rate of 30s per annum,
> for teaching Reading, writing, & Arithmetick after the rate of 20s per annum,
> to reside at Sidcott a very healthy and serene air, about twelve miles from Bristoll on the road to Exon
> Friends of the County to assure him as many schollars as will amount to £30 per annum for teaching:
> that nyne poundes per annum is proposed for Boarding such Schollars as he shall board.

At Quarterly Meeting on the 28th September 1699 Friends were told that William Jenkins was settled at Sidcot and those who wished to send their children to his school should 'as soone as they please doe the same'. Friends wasted no time in engaging his talents and at Monthly Meeting at Frome the 26th of 6th month (August) 1699, there was already the suggestion that the paper to be recorded in the front of the books for Sufferings be entered by 'Frinds schoolmaster', and in the following month it was agreed that William Jenkins 'doe begin the books of Sufferings and that Frinds doe take care to send him the booke from each Meeting'. This was the first of many writing and copying jobs which were to be given to him, presumably because of his neat copperplate writing.

Within a few months of settling at Sidcot, he married Hannah Bennet of Bristol. It did not take long for him to settle into Monthly Meeting business. In December 1699 he was already helping William Reeve and Richard Hipsley to draw up a testimony against Richard Yeape jnr. of Cheddar. In the same meeting he was to draw up a certificate of clearness for Charles Hodds who was moving to Pennsylvania. In the following month they considered methods of preventing rebellious children from going out into 'extravagant courses' and John Cowling, William Jenkins, Arthur Thomas, William Reeve or 'any Frinds that have freedom' were to plan something so that it could go to Quarterly Meeting. William Jenkins wrote a paper which was presented by William Reeve and Arthur Thomas at Quarterly Meeting, so his first six months at Sidcot were busy enough even though he may not have had many scholars.

Fitting out the school and building the schoolroom cost £13 17s, which was borne by Quarterly Meeting. In all, including the deficit for the first year, the cost to Quarterly Meeting was £29.12s.2d. Quarterly Meeting collected £22.5s. 3d, £8 of which came from the North Division and the remainder was made up with money 'that was returned from a Friend that was about to goe to Pensilvany but did not goe'. In 1701 at Quarterly Meeting, William Jenkins was 17s. 3d short of the £30 Friends had agreed so this was made up out of the Public Stock. At the corresponding Quarterly Meeting in 1702 'disbursements about the schoole house at Sydcot' came to 5s 3d and that sum was duly paid and it was the last time that William Jenkins appealed to the Quarterly Meeting for help, although Monthly Meeting 8th month 1702 'pd. Wm. Jenkins 15s for some expenditure at school'.

In 1700 William Jenkins was prosecuted by the Bishop of Bath & Wells for keeping a school without a licence. The act of James I which required that taking out a licence from the Bishop before opening a school, was directed against Catholics, but provided another weapon for use against Quakers. Although the verdict was given against William Jenkins, the conviction was set aside. Further attempts to get a conviction were made by the Sheriff of Somerset and two successive Bishops but their efforts failed and William Jenkins' school was allowed to carry on its work in peace.

For eighteen years William Jenkins carried on the work of teaching and attending meetings, visiting, drawing up certificates and testimonies, copying documents and inspecting accounts. We can get some idea of his energy from the Monthly Meeting minutes for hardly a meeting went by without his being appointed for something. Monthly Meeting was often held at his house and he was a frequent representative to Quarterly Meeting where he was in charge of ordering Friends' books from the printer. Perhaps he was taking on too much, a common occurrence with schoolmasters, and things came to a head in 1717 with an apparently trivial decision at Monthly Meeting to alter the day of the weekday meeting from 5th day to 4th day. Abraham Thomas was to acquaint Quarterly Meeting of this decision. At Quarterly Meeting, William Jenkins 'opposed Abram Thomas and signified that it was not the agreement of our Monthly Meeting and also spoke many grateing Expressions with great warmth in a disorderly manner against Abram Thomas'. He had even written a petition and had got people to sign it saying that they were not willing for the day to be altered.

When asked to come to Monthly Meeting to explain himself, he wrote that he was 'indisposed in his bodily health' but as what he wrote about the matter was not satisfactory, he was asked to come to the next Monthly Meeting. He was still 'stiff and refractory' in his behaviour, so four Friends were asked to look into the matter and make a report, which they duly did to a Monthly Meeting held at Nailsea on the 3rd of 7th mo. 1717.

It had all started when the usual enquiry was made at the Monthly Meeting before the Quarterly Meeting about how weekday meetings were kept up and 'Sidcott friends could not give so good account as they desired' because 5th day was Bristol market day and many of them had more business on that day than on any other. It was suggested that they should change the day of their meeting to 4th day 'and most agreed to it if not all except Wm. Jenkins who was there present and Friends discoursed with him the reasonableness of altering the day, he seemed passively to comply to the advice of Friends, as the Meeting thought...'. Then he turned up at Quarterly Meeting with his objections and the petition. The four Friends looked at the names on the petition and there seemed no reason why the 4th day should not have been all right for them, but not for William Jenkins who was a 'Public Friend' and would occasionally have had a clash of interest as Monthly Meeting was on 4th day. 'This is what do commonly fall to our Publick friends lotts, not to be at their own Meeting at whome and vissiting the Churches abroad at one and the same time....'. Many Friends today will know the feeling.

In 1718 he was in trouble again for complaining irregularly at Quarterly Meeting. 'Wm. Jenkins made a complaint to last Q.M. concerning some accounts of John Jenkins relating to the building of Sidcot Meeting house'. This was probably alteration to the existing building to accomodate all the scholars. The complaint was made at a very long Quarterly Meeting at Glastonbury in the 1st mo. 1718, which had to be adjourned till the evening, and the parties were advised that neither side was to present Quarterly Meeting with a paper which the other side had not seen. The complaint was referred back to Monthly Meeting and 'Wm. Jenkins is advised by this meeting to keep silent as to his Publick Preaching till such time hee is reconciled to the particular meeting to which he belongs to and also to the Monthly Meeting which hee have Quarrelled with at the Quarterly Meeting....'. John Jenkins was from Keynsham but settled in Axbridge when he married Anna Lawrence in 1705. Monthly Meeting was held at his house on the 2nd of 4th mo. 1718 and three Friends looked at the accounts and found that the meeting was £9 0s 8d in his debt. William Jenkins had refused to meet the three Friends to discuss the issue. Richard Hipsley, John Jenkins and Abraham Thomas were appointed to draw up 'a copy of defence relating to W.J.'s appeall and deliver it to him or leave it at his house'.

In the midst of all this trouble Thomas Story visited Sidcot. Thomas Story

QUAKERS AT SIDCOT

(1662-1742) came from Cumberland and was a close friend of William Penn. He travelled extensively in England and in America and on the 18th 7th mo. 1718 he arrived at Sidcot. There, as we read from his journal, 'we sat a long time before the Lord was pleased to open himself but he condescended at last and his reward came with him for we had an open time: and William Jenkins, a schoolmaster and Friend there, bringing with him all his scholars, many of them gentlemen's sons about the country, I had something for them in particular'.

He was joined later by Samuel Bownas (1676-1753) who had already visited Sidcot in 1699-1700. Samuel Bownas was a blacksmith's apprentice who became a powerful Quaker minister. He also came from Cumberland but settled in Limington and so was a member of Quarterly Meeting. It seems he was not popular with William Jenkins at that time, as at the long Quarterly Meeting at Glastonbury referred to above, William Jenkins objected that Samuel Bownas was not fit to judge in the case. Other representatives disagreed, but the whole discussion was obviously taking too long and it was postponed until the next Quarterly Meeting when, however, William Jenkins did not turn up. On the 25th September, Samuel Bownas and Thomas Story went together to the Quarterly Meeting to which the latter refers as being 'large and open'. He goes on to write 'Here we reconciled a difference that had been long depending between a Friend and a Monthly Meeting, which had done much hurt among them and all ended in peace and satisfaction'.

The following Monthly Meeting at Weston 6th of 8th mo. 1718, William Jenkins signed a statement to the effect that 'the Controversies and differences are finally Concluded and ended and to be mentioned no More, Provided the said Wm. Jenkins doe continue to behave himselfe a Friend of Peace, and as becomes a minister of Christ'.

Meanwhile the school was obviously doing well. 'The gentlemen's sons about the country' were not all members of the Society. Bristol Quarterly Meeting, in answer to a Query from Yearly Meeting signified that there were children of people from different persuasions who attended and went to meetings. Children of poor Friends were not forgotten and William Jenkins offered in 1701 to board them free if Monthly Meeting were to pay for their teaching. In 1719 Northern Monthly Meeting agreed to place Mary Pitstow's son Isaac, of Frome, at the school for six months to be taught reading, writing and arithmetic. He was to be paid for by the Meeting which would also provide clothing. This was so that he could be apprenticed, which he was in the 6th mo. 1720 to Thomas Greenhill of Bath. He became a prominent member of Bath Meeting in later years.

The peace between William Jenkins and Monthly Meeting did not last. The cause of the ill feeling was an obscure dispute between William Jenkins and his nephew Webb Davis. Monthly Meeting was not particularly interested in hearing the details of the complaint as we read in the minutes of 1st of 1st mo. 1725 that 'some months past Will Jenkins offered to read a paper at the end of

INTO THE EIGHTEENTH CENTURY

our then meeting but the time being far spent Friends was not willing to be incomoded in their going home at which hee then signified hee would apeal to the Quarter Meeting where he offered it but it was turned back to our meeting, and hee at this time offered again to read the said paper wee did not agree for him to read it, but signified that if he would deliver us his paper it should bee read and hee should have it againe or a coppy thereof with our answer thereto, but he would not comply to nothing but his own reading of it which was not admited'. William Jenkins took this to heart and felt that Monthly Meeting was excluding him.

On 24th 1st mo. 1726, Quarterly Meeting again lasted for hours, in fact it was adjourned until the following morning at 7.00a.m.! Having heard both William Jenkins and representatives of Monthly Meeting, friends of Quarterly Meeting found no substance in William Jenkins' accusations that the Monthly Meeting was trying to exclude him, and he was told to burn all the notes and papers he had written. This he refused to do and appealed to Yearly Meeting in London. The clerks were to give him a copy of the committee's opinion, and prepare another copy for Quarterly Meeting representatives to take to Yearly Meeting.

The committee appointed by Yearly Meeting found the 'difference very slender' and also told him to destroy the papers. This time he complied but did not attend Monthly Meeting again until 5th of 4th mo. 1727 after submitting a paper signed by Webb Davis 'that the affaire between him and his uncle shall be at a final end'.

At Monthly Meeting in Bath 1st mo. 1729 we read that William Jenkins had sold his estate and required a certficate. He moved to Bristol and died there in 1735. His colourful personality must have been missed at Sidcot. He was a successful schoolmaster and 29 years was long time to be running a school. However, this area was not long without a school for, at a meeting at Joseph Bryant's in the 1st mo. 1730, it was reported that Jonah Thompson of Westmorland was come to settle in Yatton 'to teach a schoole'.

POOR FRIENDS AT SIDCOT

William Watts
William and Rebecca Watts lived at Nempnett so they were probably connected with Chew Meeting as well as Sidcot, though when mentioned in the Quarterly Meeting minutes of 1668, William Watts is clearly of Burrington Meeting. He was obviously a friend of William Reeve, who took him £1 from Timothy Willis' will and left him £2 in his own as mentioned already, although the gift money was usually delivered by John Hipsley or John Lovell of Chew. In 1712 'William Watts, an ancient Friend and his wife' were advised to move nearer a meeting 'that in their Old Age they may have some society with Friends'. They agreed

to take this advice, but Friends were desired to remind them occasionally. They were reminded from time to time, and always agreed, but never seemed to get round to moving. Their daughter, Mary, married William Stringer in 1715, in Chew Meeting House. Rebecca turned up at Portishead to Monthly Meeting on 4th of 4th mo. 1716. She agreed to sell their house and Friends proposed to provide a house for them in Portishead. She was given 10s to take away. In the 7th mo. 1721 'Will Watts and wife being very antient Friends and shee very weak and sick, it is agreed to send them out of our stock for their reliefe 08s 0d by John Hipsley', so presumably they had not moved yet. They continued to receive money until 1729 when William Watts was mentioned for the last time.

Sarah Beess
Sarah Brodman was married to Richard Beess in Winscombe Church in 1664, but she obviously became associated with Friends. In 1699 'Wm. Lovell being present gives account to this meeting of the great poverty of Sarah Beess of Berrington, and its left to the said Wm. Lovell and his brother to endevour what they can with the parish for their reliefe, and the Friends do also allow her something as they se meet'. In the 11th mo. 1699 we read 'item, to Wm. Lovell for the relife of Sara Beess to relive her as a poor woman that coms sometimes amongst frinds 2s 6d'. She generally received 2s 6d a month, plus extra towards buying her some clothes. Then in 1st mo. 1705 'gave to Sarah Beeses to buy her som bedcloathes by John Lovell 5s' and in 4th mo. 1705 'to Sarah Beeses by Tho. Davis by reason of her illness 2s 6d'. It looks as if she died soon after this last entry.

Mary Hucker
Mary Hucker of Worle, widow of John Hucker, seems to have been looked after by Sidcot Friends. In 10th mo. 1713 she was in debt and Sidcot Friends were advised to speak with her, and 'advise her to let her creditors know how it is with her' and offer everything to them. On the 4th of the 11th mo. 1713 at Monthly Meeting at Chew she agreed to take Friends advice. At the same meeting, there was a letter from John Whiting jnr. in London saying that he had received the letter from Abraham Thomas on behalf of Grace, daughter of Mary Hucker. He wrote that he would 'take care of her if friends will send her up to London free from charge and well clothed'. Accordingly the meeting appointed some Friends to see what clothing she needed and provide it for her. The cost came to £3.0s.10d. which was more that the 40s. upper limit originally set by the meeting, but it was paid and Grace Hucker went to London.

An interesting medical aside was mentioned in the minutes of Monthly Meeting 2nd mo. 1717:

> To Mary Hucker for to pay the doctor towards setting her heep bone —
> £2 10s 0d   note the Doctors demand is four guineys

INTO THE EIGHTEENTH CENTURY

(Compare that with one half year's rent of Alice Dogget's house 13s or ten copies of Thomas Ellwood's books bought by Sidcot Meeting for £1.10s)

Gabriell Ballet

Gabriell Ballet's marriage to Mary Tugwell of Winscombe in 1691 was probably the first in Sidcot Meeting House. In 1700 he was prosecuted by the Parson of Wedmore for refusing to pay ten years of Easter-Offerings. These amounted to 9d per annum and his non-payment resulted in a gaol sentence. In 1709 we hear of him again: 'Gabriell Ballet a poor friend that belongs to Glaston Monthly Meeting being at Sidcott have meett with an accident and broak his legg, Friends have sent him as a token of our love in his present necessity 5s by Wm. Jenkins'.

Jane Hardige

On the 7th 12th mo. 1714 we come across a Friend who was to become the most interesting 'poor' Friend of Sidcot Meeting, although at the time when she was about to be married she was not thinking of problems to come. George Hardige of Sidcot proposed marriage to Jane Gardner of Axbridge and, when it was published at Sidcot Meeting, no objections were raised. They were married at Sidcot Meeting early in 1715, but married happiness did not last. While Jane was busy with the children, George fell into 'vain company'. At Monthly Meeting in the 7th mo. 1721 report was made that he had 'been guilty of frequent drunkenness for which he have been often dealt with'. He was not willing to give up his evil practice and John Jenkins and Richard Hipsley were to let him know that he was desired to go to the next meeting. At Nailsea on 2nd 8th mo. 1721 he did come but 'appeared in a hard and conceited frame of spirit' so Friends felt it their duty to testify against him. The testimony was drawn up by the following month and read to George and then again in Sidcot Meeting. That is the last we hear of George Hardige.

At Nailsea in the 8th mo. 1726 Jane Hardige and her children were reported to be in a sick and weak condition. Richard Hipsley, John Jenkins and Abraham Thomas were appointed to visit the family and relieve them if they found it neccessary. From then on Jane Hardige features regularly as the recipient of charity money. For example she received 12s 6d. from John Jenkins' legacy in 3rd mo. 1728. In 11th mo. 1728 Wm. Jenkins was given 11s 6d which he had already paid out for her, but this was not encouraged and it was 'desired that this may not be a president for the future'. But she was obviously in trouble as in the 12th mo. 1728 she was said to owe the landlord about £5 rent. Richard Hipsley and Abraham Thomas were appointed to see what she had that could be sold to pay him, and also to consider where she and her children could go for the following year. The following month she and her family moved into Sidcot Meeting House.

Lodging poor Friends in Meeting Houses was a common practice, but this was the first time we hear of anyone living in Sidcot Meeting House. Until recently before that time, Shusan Brodmore had lodged at Claverham, but being weak and lame, was moved to a more convenient place (12th mo. 1728). Mary Cuffe, who was a poor Friend and had lived at Belluton Meeting House, was murdered in 1727.

Jane Hardige received about 10s a month plus money from legacies. In the 8th mo. 1729 we read: 'sent to Jane Hardidge two pounds of Will Edwards annual legacy in order to pay John Hill surgeon for a cure don to one of her sons'.

In 1730 we start to read the saga of Jane's children. Her daughter, who had been in service in Bristol returned to her mother at Sidcot, but Monthly Meeting did not think it advisable in her 'present circumstances to keep her daughter with her' and Richard Marchant of Bath promised he would find a place for her. This he did, and she was placed at John Cowling's, but she didn't stay long. On the 4th of 11th mo. 1730 'Jane Hardige's daughter was sent to Bath as proposed at last meeting and placed to John Cowling but the girle is gon from her place and her Master knows not whether, soe if shee returns to her Mother at Sidcott friends are to take due care as may be proper and report their answer next meeting'. The next meeting 'we hear that Jane Hardige's daughter is com home to her Grandfather at Chedar'. I hope she was allowed to stay, as she was obviously not happy so far away from home.

Next, it was the boys' turn. They were aged about eight and nine when in 1732 it was proposed 'Jane Hardige two boys to be offered to our next Quarter Meeting for to be placed to James Fell to be boarded and kept to scoole if approved of. Abram Thomas and Richd. Hipsley is ordered to gett such necessary Clothing for them as needfull'. James Fell of Glastonbury had recently married Grace Thomas, Abraham's daughter, so no doubt she offered to keep an eye on them. They were accordingly clothed and sent to school and the bill for their clothing amounted to £2.13s. About a year later, they needed some more shirts: 'Jas. Bryant to send their mother Cloth to make them each two shirts a piece and to bring his bill to our next meeting'. These four shirts cost 7s.9d. There was another bill for clothes paid to James Fell £1.6s.9d, presumably to clothe them suitably to be sent to Bath, where they were taken early in 1734 by Richard Marchant. They were taken to the Widow Collet of Bathford and Peter Berry of Bath Easton, both clothiers. As the boys were both so young, George still only eleven and William ten, it was considered that they should be placed until they were fourteen and then apprenticed. If their master or mistress did not agree to apprentice them, then they should be paid 20s a year towards their maintenance and clothing. If they were to be bound as apprentices, then Half Year Meeting allowed £6 for each boy. However, Peter Berry decided within a month that he didn't want William, so Edward Marchant proposed that his son John Marchant should take William on the same terms. (Half Year Meeting was responsible for apprenticeships, schooling, and finance in general. They published a list of 'objects' — poor people who were 'suitable objects of our care'.)

INTO THE EIGHTEENTH CENTURY

William stuck it out longer than George, who ran away after a year and nine months. William stayed with John Marchant for three years, then William Seldon of Bath, rough mason, was persuaded to take him for £6 on a month's trial. William Hardige was bound to William Seldon and his indentures were taken to Half Year Meeting where they were paid and deposited in the chest and John Marchant was paid £3. However, all was not plain sailing as William Hardige ran away to his mother six months later. The last we hear in the minutes is that William Frampton and John Lovell were desired to speak to William Hardige to persuade him to go back to his master who was ready to receive him, but they failed to persuade him to return. That was in 1739, and after this the Hardige family mysteriously disappear from the minutes and Jane is no longer on the list of 'objects' from Half Year Meeting. It was as if they had never existed.

TRAVELLING FRIENDS

Apart from visiting Samuel Bownas, who became a member of Quarterly Meeting when he settled at Limington (near Ilchester), Thomas Story paid several visits to Friends in the area including the Vickris family at Chew. After visiting Elizabeth Vickris on the 27th 5th mo. 1722 he records that 'on 29th I went to Sidcot weekday meeting where the Lord was pleased to favour us with his presence to a good degree'. The following month, on the 13th, the Quarterly Meeting for Somerset was held at Taunton.

On the next morning, 'accompanied by a Friend belonging to Sidcot Meeting, I set forward towards Bridgewater'. About three miles from Taunton, they met three companies of footsoldiers who had come over from Ireland and were marching to Exeter. Having passed 'and riding near the hedge, we suddenly met a footman in white, leading a dog, which so scared my horse, that he flounced round and jumped to the other side of the lane, by which he threw me out of the stirrups and upon the pummel of the saddle. Finding himself loose, he ran back towards Taunton, so that I could by no means turn or stop him or recover the stirrups or saddle. Coming up with the rear of the soldiers, I called to them to stop him if they could'. Although they tried with their muskets and staffs they couldn't stop him but it slowed the horse enough for Thomas Story to jump off. The horse set one foot on his temple and another on his chest. He was not too badly injured, at least he thought not, and rejected the officers' idea of sending for a doctor. He started to walk, not willing to remount his horse until it had got over its excitement, but feeling faint, he had to sit down by the side of the road. He became more conscious of his hurt 'and putting my hand to the side of my head, found it wounded and bloody, which the Friend perceiving, shook his head and turned pale, supposing it worse than it was'. Gradually Thomas Story's strength returned and in about half an hour he was ready to set out again. The Sidcot Friend rode Thomas Story's horse and they rode very slowly and got cold. The next day he was stiff all over with bruises, but went to all the meetings he was expecting to attend, unhindered by his injuries. He felt he had had a miraculous escape. The Sidcot Friend must have been Abraham Thomas, as he was the only one from Sidcot present at that particular Quarterly Meeting. Thomas Story stayed at Bridgewater till the 18th, then on to Mark, then to William Jenkins'.

In 1729 Isaac Sharples came to live in the area. He was a traveller and wished to visit meetings in Wales, North of England and Scotland, and asked Monthly Meeting for a certificate. It was discussed at Portishead, Claverham and Sidcot Meetings, and granted the following month. Isaac Sharples had a successful tour and returned in the 9th mo. 1730. He also visited Friends in South Wales and meetings in and around London on separate occasions. In 1734 he married Hester Thurston of Thornbury and shortly afterwards moved to Frenchay.

John Fothergill (whose son was one of the Friends instrumental in founding Ackworth School) came from Yorkshire and visited Sidcot and Bridgwater Meetings on successive days in 1733. John Griffith, of Darby (Pennsylvania), was a native of South Wales who emigrated to America with his parents at the age of 13 in 1726. His visit to England in 1748 was preceded by high adventure. He was captured by a privateer who took him to France and Spain before he managed to escape! He records his visit to Sidcot by noting that 'on third-day we had a very open serviceable meeting at Sidcot; the testimony of Truth flowed forth freely to the several states of those present'.

Ruth Follows from Weston in Nottinghamshire visited several times in the 1770s and 80s and records after a visit in 1773 that 'on first-day were at their meetings at Sidcot, where we were again refreshed together, though amongst a poor company'. She was one of the Friends who visited nearly all the meetings in England before her death at the age of 91.

John Churchman from Chester County, Pennsylvania, visited in the early 1750s and notes that he had good meetings at Claverham, Sidcot and Mark. He was a friend of John Woolman and visited slave-owning Friends with him. Patience Brayton came from Swansey in Massachusetts. She and her husband had been amongst the first Friends there to set their slaves free. She also visited nearly all the meetings in England and Ireland between 1784 and 1788. On her return journey, the ship sailed into a violent storm which resulted in her suffering a dislocated wrist. Another visitor from America was Henry Hull from Stanford in the State of New York, who was in England between 1810 and 1812.

Mary Dudley from Bristol writes of her visit in 1798: 'I felt increasingly drawn towards some little places in the north division of this county, and on the 3rd of the third month proceeded to Sidcot, where I sat an exercising meeting with Friends, under a deep sense of the want of life, and prevalence of an indolent unconcerned spirit... After a time of silent travail, strength being communicated, a little relief was obtained, and clearness of feeling in appointing a meeting for the next morning of a more general kind'. She moved on to a meeting at John Naish's in Congresbury in the evening, returning to Sidcot next morning to the appointed meeting, which was 'large and quiet ... and that spirit

INTO THE EIGHTEENTH CENTURY

which breathes peace on earth and good will to men happily prevailed. We dined at the school and had a solemn season before we left it, several precious young people being present'. The next day, she visited Langford and was offered rooms at the inn, where she could hold a public meeting, and then spent a few 'pleasant and solid hours' with John Thomas and Sarah Squire at Winthill.

There were, of course, other visiting Friends, many of them not recorded. Their visits must have been spiritually warming occasions, particularly for rural communities which must have felt isolated at times. They were also a source of Quakerly news in the days before 'The Friend'.

Gossip

In 1726 James Coomer of Cheddar, for several years regular at Sidcot Meeting, was married by a priest. He was asked to come to Monthly Meeting, but made excuses for several months. Eventually, six months later, he did come and tender 'advice and counsell' was given him. He would not come again, so he was recorded 'out of unity with Friends'. However, it did not stop him leaving a legacy of £40 when he died in 1734 'the interest thereof to remain towards the repairation of Sidcott Meeting House for ever'.

Ann Lovell, widow of John Lovell of Wrington, had a large stone erected on her husband's grave in 1728 at Claverham. This 'brought a great uneasiness on divers Friends'. Friends were appointed to let her know that it was not allowed, and tell her 'to remove it speedily'. She agreed, and it was removed.

In the same year Elizabeth Webb (not from Sidcot) was married by a priest. She had already been warned against marrying the man two years previously, but it must have been true love, as she was willing to face being rejected by Friends. However, either the Friends who were appointed to speak to her saw how deep her feelings were, or she knew how to cajole them. John Hipsley and Richard Hipsley gave 'account that they have spoak with Eliz. Web and she seemed to receive their vissett lovingly and signified that she hoped she shold gaine Friends love towards her againe, its the judgement of this meeting not to be concerned any further with her'. They added various pious warnings to young people not to go to the priest to be married, and earnest desires that Friends should watch over them, but they left it at that without actually disowning her.

Robert Spender was a minister of Sidcot Meeting when he was accused by his servant of having had 'too familiar Conversation with Her...'. His continued silence about the affair condemned him and he was disowned by Monthly Meeting, although they expressed regrets. That was in 1746, and in 1752 he applied to be reinstated but he was not allowed back into the fold.

In 1765 there was an irregular marriage at Claverham between William Heath of Bristol and Martha Wilmott of Claverham. When their proposals of marriage were rejected, they just turned up in meeting on first day and took each other in marriage. Some of the Friends of Claverham were also at fault, as were some members of Frenchay Monthly Meeting, for signing the certificate. This was frowned on by the Public Friends of Monthly Meeting, but there was obviously some feeling of sympathy in Claverham Meeting, which could not have escaped attention at Sidcot.

In 1777 Martha Curtis was married by a priest, and became Martha Derrick. Richard Manfield and John Thomas, who were requested to visit on this occasion, said 'she seemed sensibly affected concerning her past conduct....and will be ready to condemn it at some future time.' Sure enough, two months later, she did. The couple lived at Max Mills, in the Parish of Winscombe, and had six children. The mother wanted them educated in the ways of Friends, to which her husband did not object, 'yet this meeting on considering their case, seems most easy to suspend the accepting of the children as members of our Society for the present.' Why? Was there a question of money involved somewhere? It was not cheap educating six children, especially as they would have had to go to Ackworth, and Martha was already receiving charity anyway.

In 7th mo. 1799 a Committee composed of both men and women friends was appointed to look into 'whether our several mtgs for worship are held at such hours as leave the body most free from a Propensity for drowsiness.' The 'drowsiness committee' duly met and considered there should be no change in the times of meetings for the time being.

John Horsington Grigg was the son of Prudence Grigg, an overseer of Sidcot Meeting. In 3rd mo. 1808 he was reported to have been drinking to excess and also was intending to marry someone not belonging to the Society of Friends. Thomas Tanner and Joseph Naish were requested to visit. Their report reads:

> We have had an interview with John Horsington Grigg who readily gave us his company and did not deny several of the charges laid against him such as drinking to access, singing, dancing and associating himself with improper company, neither did he attempt to justify his conduct therein, but acknowledged it to be wrong and hoped that he should be more careful in future yet he acknowledged that there was a connection between him and a young woman not of our society relative to marriage and that he could not at present say that he had any inclination to give it up .

He seems like an honest young man, and the visit may have had some effect on him as we read later that he gave up seeing the young woman, and when he moved to Wellington his conduct improved and he became more frequent in attending Meetings. Something must have happened, though, as he was described as 'not a member' when he died in 1865.

INTO THE EIGHTEENTH CENTURY

Preparative Meetings

The Quarterly Meeting recommended the setting up of Preparative Meetings in 1777 long before it was mentioned at Yearly Meeting in 1794. They were to be held at the close of the meeting before Monthly Meeting, not necessarily on First Day though. At Monthly Meeting in 12th mo. 1788 it was agreed that Preparative Meetings should be held in order, and Sidcot's was to be on 6th day, which was the day of the weekday meetings. At the Yearly Meeting in 1794 it was agreed that the holding of Preparative Meetings could be helpful, and that the proper business of such meetings was:-

> To inquire after births, burials, and removals, in order to carry accounts thereof to the monthly meeting:
>
> To read and consider the queries, as settled by the yearly meeting, and conclude on answers to them, except to the eleventh, twelfth, fourteenth, and the latter part of the thirteenth; in writing if convenient:
>
> To appoint representatives to the monthly meeting.
>
> If overseers or other concerned friends incline to consult the preparative meeting, before they report cases of delinquency to the monthly meeting, they may do so; but the preparative meeting should not make a record thereof.

At the same Quarterly Meeting in 1777 it was decided that friends were also to appoint Overseers 'either men or women or both as it best suits' for each Particular Meeting. It was at Monthly Meeting in 8th mo. 1757 that Sidcot's first overseers were appointed. They were, of course, Richard Hispley and John Thomas.

We saw that William Jenkins was a 'Publick Friend'. They soon began to be called 'ministers' and were recorded as such in the Monthly Meeting minutes. This was not to say that nobody else could say anything in meeting for worship, nor were they paid, it was just recognised that they had a particular gift. They were also encouraged to travel 'in the ministry', and this was a good way of keeping up with the news of what was going on in other parts of the country. The practice of recording ministers was continued until London Yearly Meeting in 1924. Elders were concerned with the spiritual welfare of the meeting, and overseers with the pastoral care. Overseers were first appointed in 1757. At first there did not appear to be much difference between the two offices.

At the Select Meeting of Ministers and Elders, held at Joseph Naish's in Congresbury the ministers and elders had an opportunity to discuss the Quarterly Meeting queries. After a time of silence, they considered the queries and answered them in writing. They also had time to discuss any problems which might have arisen. These meetings were the precursors of our elders' and overseers' meetings.

QUAKERS AT SIDCOT

The Hipsley Family
We have already met the first Richard Hipsley of Stock, in the parish of Churchill. He and his wife Hannah left six children:

Hannah	b. 1700
Ann	b. 1701
Mary	
John	b. 1703
Sarah	b. 1705
Richard	b. 1708 (Hannah died when he was a year old).

Young Hannah married Richard Thomas at Sidcot in 1726. She became a member of Portishead meeting, and was regularly at Monthly Meeting, when the women's Monthly Meetings were re-established in 1755.

Mary married James Wreach in 1721, but not without a small problem on the way. James Wreach's mother would not give her consent until her husband made some settlement on their other children, which he did intend to do, in time. James was advised to wait and 'endeavour to prevail with his mother.' However, all settlements were quickly made and James and Mary were married at Sidcot.

John does not seem to have had the privileges which might have been expected by the oldest son. He married Mary Thomas at Claverham in 1733, and then settled in Wrington, and was an active member of Claverham meeting.

Richard, who married in 1738 Ann Salter of Puddimore, seems to have inherited the farm at Stock. The list of his 'sufferings' for each year include:

3cwt cheese	£3.10.9.
Beasts	£5. 6.0.
2 Hogsheads full cider	£4.15.0.
Yoke of Stears	£4. 4.3.
Cheese and wool	£3.16.6.
3 Hogsheads and 13 gallons cider	£4. 1.6.

Why were 3 Hogsheads and 13 gallons of cider worth less than 2 Hogsheads? You may wonder what Richard Hipsley was doing making cider anyway, but at that time it was a much safer drink than water and Friends were only disapproved of if they drank too much too often! They sometimes had an adjourned meeting at a convenient inn, and many breweries were owned by Friends.

Richard Hipsley first spoke in ministry when he was thirty five and soon became an able minister. He visited Ireland, London, Dorset, Worcestershire, Herefordshire, and Wiltshire. His testimony describes him as having a cheerful disposition, and as being a kind neighbour, always ready to help those around him. He must have been missed at Sidcot when he died in 1767.

Ann is mentioned in the minutes of the revived women's Monthly Meeting. In 12th mo. 1755 she was Sidcot Meeting's representative to Quarterly Meeting, and she also delivered some charity money to Mary Pow. She outlived her husband by twelve years.

Richard and Ann had in all eight children but not all survived infancy.

Mary	b. 25-1-1740	
John	b. 21-2-1741	
Richard	b. 19-8-1742	
Ann	b. 26-2-1744	died as a baby.
Ann	b. 9-6-1746	
Samuel	b. 29-7-1748	
Robert	b. 14th July 1753	d. Oct. 1753
James	b. 14th July 1753	d. Oct. 1753

Mary married William Phippen of Bristol, at Sidcot, in 1764, and both parents were present at Monthly Meeting to give their consent.

John married Elizabeth Selfe in 1762 and there were eight children, only two of whom, Hannah and John, survived infancy. They lived in Bristol for a while then, when John's father died, they moved back into the Monthly Meeting area with his brother Samuel as his apprentice. He became an invaluable member of Claverham meeting, becoming an Elder in 1771. In 1767, the same year he moved back into the area, John Hipsley bought some mills in Congresbury, and when he sold them in 1790, to John Naish, he was described as a baker of Congresbury. In 1791 he was appointed as Superintendent of Ackworth School. He left in 1795, a gratuity of 200 guineas being given to him by the Committee of the school.

Ann never married. She is described as Ann Hipsley of Stock when she died in 1802 aged 56. Samuel moved to Melksham in 1771 when he married Lydia Jefferies there.

It was Richard who again seems to have inherited the farm. Like his father he was fairly regular at Monthly Meeting until about 1779, the year his mother died. Then in 5th mo. 1784 it was reported that he had been married by a priest. He and his first cousin, Betty Palmer, had obviously fallen in love and rather than give each other up they had gone to a priest to be married. They knew that it was impossible that Quakers would allow such a thing, because to them even marriage between second cousins was anathema, except in very exceptional circumstances. John Thomas and Richard Manfield paid a visit to them and 'neither of them expressed so satisfactory respecting their past misconduct as could be wished,' so John Thomas and John Benwell were asked to draw up a Testimony of Denial against Richard. They were also to send a copy of the

Meeting's proceedings to Middle Division where his wife came from. This they did, and Thomas Tanner was asked to deliver a copy to him, and to read it publicly at the close of a meeting for worship at Sidcot.

We next hear of the family in 1803, nearly twenty years later, when John Benwell 'reports that the preparative meeting of Sidcot wishes to recommend Richard Hipsley Jnr. (son of Richard and Betty) to the Notice of Friends we therefore appoint Joseph Naish and Edward Gregory to pay him a visit and report to next Meeting.'

By the next month, 30/1/1804, the Friends brought their report in which they thought Richard did not show 'as much sensibility about him as could have been wished'. Nevertheless, they thought he did require 'the tender care and sympathy of his friends.' He applied for membership again in 1808 and this time he was admitted. The minutes refer to Rule 11, Page 111, Book of Extracts, and it was the first time that Rules had been referred to in this way. This particular rule concerned the children of disowned parents. It was felt that Richard deserved to be admitted having obviously attended meeting regularly from childhood, but the Monthly Meeting still had doubts. Doubts which were realised in 1814 when Richard Hipsley was accused of immoral conduct. At first he denied it, but then admitted that the young woman in question was going to have his child. After all, she had sworn it before the magistrate, so Richard agreed to pay her maintenance, but was immediately disowned by Friends.

Meanwhile Betty and Richard, who had been disowned in 1784, were applying to be reinstated. They had obviously been attending meeting regularly since their marriage, and were reinstated immediately. Perhaps Friends had persuaded them to re-apply because they were having money problems, as at the following share out of charity money on 30/1/1815 'Richard Hipsley & wife' received £8.0.0.. Richard Hipsley again appeared on the list of representatives at Monthly Meeting.

Betty Hipsley died in 1820 and Richard, now an old man, could not manage.

Richard Hipsley handed over his estate to his son for an annuity for life of £15 and had it legally conveyed. Friends thought it too little, but Richard thought he was doing the right thing. The son offered to board him for £10 per year to be paid for by the Monthly Meeting! However, Richard was happy to be with his son in the same house in which he had always lived. He died shortly after this, however, and in 6th mo. 1820 he is referred to as 'the late Richard Hipsley'.

INTO THE EIGHTEENTH CENTURY

John Thomas
We now meet the man who was to be the backbone of Sidcot Meeting throughout most of the eighteenth century. He was born about 1714, grandson of Arthur and Lydia Thomas, son of Abraham and Grace, and uncle to many of the Tanner family whom we shall meet later. He was married to Sarah Perris of Long Sutton in 1738, the same year in which Richard Hipsley was married. He was also a yeoman, and he also refused to pay tithes and church rates.

In 1753 he had cattle worth £8.0s.8d taken from him. In 1757 John Thomas' sufferings amounted to

11 bushels of wheat worth	£4.12s.10d
1 heifer and calf "	£5. 2s. 6d
4 bushels of wheat "	12s. 0d.

In 1769 John Thomas reported 'that he hath transcribed the minutes of this Meeting for the last year in the mo. meeting book....' He continued as clerk of Monthly Meeting for at least ten years. He was also Monthly Meeting treasurer for about forty five years! His writing was very neat and legible.

In 2nd. mo. 1770 it was reported to the Monthly Meeting that 'severall persons about Sidcott have frequented that Meeting for some time...' John Hipsley, Wm. Tanner, and John Thomas were appointed to visit. Thomas Tanner was admitted at this time, and three months later he was married to Sarah Curtis, a member of Sidcot Meeting. Sarah Syms 'a young woman of Banwell...' was also admitted. She eventually married, in 1787, Joseph Gillett a shopkeeper of Somerton, in Sidcot Meeting House.

John Thomas was extremely faithful in his attendance at Monthly Meetings and Quarterly Meetings. He was present almost every month even when the attendance at Monthly Meeting was very low, which it was throughout the middle of the eighteenth century. Throughout the whole of 1747 there was a maximum of ten at Monthly Meeting, and sometimes as few as five. In 1756, after the resumption of the women's meeting, the attendance at the men's Monthly Meeting was up a little. Perhaps the wives and sisters wanted to go, and persuaded the men!

Since the answers to the Quarterly Meeting queries were not satisfactory in 1782 a committee was set up to report on the state of individual meetings. They made their report in 11th mo. 1782, and this is what they said about Sidcot:-

> Sidcot, which meeting is but small, yet the Friends who constitute it, seem, in general, of reputable conduct, externally supporting a religious Character & some few among them evidently appear to us to be truly religiously concerned & we wish there was no Room to suspect that Regularity of Conduct has been substituted by any in the Room of Real, vital, experimental Religion.

This diplomatic minute leaves the spiritual state of the meeting at that time very much to our imagination.

Portishead was made up of very few Friends, mainly women. Claverham was fairly large, as was Bath, but the committee was not satisfied with Bath Friends. Belluton was very small, but faithful, and Hallatrow consisted mainly of attenders. The members of the committee who signed the report were John Thomas from Sidcot, Richard Manfield from Claverham, Robert Bishop from Chew, John Hipsley from Claverham and John Benwell from Sidcot.

In 1786 John Thomas had a concern to accompany his friend Thomas Melhuish of Taunton on a religious visit to friends in Devonshire. The Monthly Meeting approved and gave him a minute 'signd on Behalf of the meeting which may also serve to inform friends of that Part that he is of an exemplary Conduct and Conversation & that his ministry is acceptable to us.' Another visit he made was to Friends in Cornwall which he accomplished with a 'degree of satisfaction'. Thomas Melhuish visited a Monthly Meeting at Sidcot on his way to visit families of friends, and John Thomas was 'set at liberty' to go with him.

When John Thomas died in 1802 he was buried at Claverham Burial Ground. He had been a minister for twenty eight years. This is how friends described him:-

> This our antient and honorable Friend was favored through a long course of years to live a pious and exemplary Life, his diffident disposition added to a becoming Gravity of Deportment greatly endeared him to his Friends, by whom he was considered as an Ornament to his Profession. (i.e. Quakerism) The few words he had occasionally to offer in meetings were acceptable as they often tended to Edification. He departed this Life in a quiet frame of mind and we doubt not is entered into the mansions of everlasting Rest.

John Thomas was evidently a 'plain' Friend, 'pious', 'exemplary' and 'grave'. What was meant by this is difficult to imagine today. His home would contain no pictures, ornaments, musical instruments or books apart from those approved by Friends. The Bible held pride of place, followed by devotional works, the journals of travelling Friends, and various tracts and pamphlets. He would not go to fairs nor other places of so called amusement which were popular at the time. He would certainly never attend cock fighting, bear baiting nor bull baiting. In fact he would not wish to do anything that would divert him from the Truth, so I imagine him sitting at his desk writing minutes or certificates, riding across the countryside to deliver some charity money, or perhaps some bad news in the way of a 'minute of disunion'. Indeed, it would seem that all his time which was not taken up by the business of overseeing his estate was spent in some work for the Quakers.

INTO THE EIGHTEENTH CENTURY

From the Yearly Meeting epistle, 1753:

> It is a matter of exceeding grief and concern to many of the faithful among us, to observe, how far that exemplary plainess of habit (clothes), speech, and deportment, which distinguished our forefathers, and for which they patiently underwent reproach and contradiction, is now departed from, by too many under our name. A declension from the simplicity of truth hath been, and we fear is, attended with pernicious consequences, in opening the way of some, the more easily and unobserved, to attend the places of public resort, for the exercise of sports, plays, and other hurtful and destructive diversions of the age; from which truth taught our faithful elders, and still teaches us, wholly to refrain:........Wherefore, we beseech you, be not deceived, nor led aside by false notions of imaginary pleasure, to partake of "the unfruitful works of darkness," but watch and be sober; and, as becometh children of the light and of the day, "Abstain from all appearance of evil'". Eph.5 v.11; 1 Thess. 5 v.5,6,22

John Thomas obviously took this advice to heart.

Martha Vowles and Charles Strode

In 10th. mo. 1780 it was reported at Monthly Meeting that Martha Vowles, a girl of about fifteen from Wrington, was provided with a place of servitude, but was badly off for clothing. Robert Bishop was to request women Friends to buy her some more.

In 5th. mo. 1788 Martha Vowles was said to be 'keeping company with a man not of our society' and was likely to be married soon. When Martha was visited she received her visitors very kindly but did not seem likely to put a stop to her plans for her marriage. Perhaps she was planning something else!

In 2nd.mo. 1790 Charles Strode applied for membership but was rejected, but nothing daunted, he tried again a year later, and was accepted. At a Monthly Meeting held at Claverham on   4th.mo. 1791 he was present to hear the following;

> Charles Strode of Stone Allerton in this County, Taylor, Son of Charles Strode late of the City of Bristol and Ann his wife both deceased & Martha Vowles daughter of Joseph Vowles late of Wrington but now of Stone Allerton, Taylor, & Mary his wife deceased, appearing here have signified their intentions of taking each other in marriage....

This was to be read in both Claverham and Sidcot meetings. In June they were married at last, the marriage having taken place at Claverham Meeting House.

Charles and Martha had at least ten children, most of whom attended Sidcot School although the oldest went to Ackworth and the second was sent to a girl's school at Wellington. Francis Knight in his History of Sidcot School mentions that he once met an Old Scholar of the school who could remember a son of Charles and Martha being killed in the machinery of a well there, in about 1820.

Charles and Martha moved to a thatched cottage which occupied nearly the same site as Rose Cottage does today. Charles was tailor to the school and undertook to make the boys' suits for 19s per suit, finding everything except the material. He also served as chemist and postmaster as well. Charles Strode was also a very faithful Friend, attending Monthly Meetings regularly, and also receiving about £10 charity money every six months while his children were little. When the Meeting wanted to raise money for the new Meeting House he bought from them a plot of land called Jenkins' Plot, lying near Woodborough lane in Winscombe for £20.

Martha died in 1830, Charles in 1834, and in 1835 the cottage was bought for £250 by the school, who were well aware that it was more than it was worth but they regarded the possession of it as essential. Mary Strode, daughter of Charles and Martha, wanted to marry George Smith, a shopkeeper of Axbridge, so he applied to become a member. Thus the daughter was following in her mother's footsteps in bringing her husband-to-be into the membership of the Society. They were married on 28th of the 3rd. mo. 1821. There are a number of the Strode family buried in the Sidcot Burial Ground.

John Benwell
We first hear of John Benwell when he moved to Bath from Godalming in 2nd mo. 1768. He did not remain long in the area as he had moved away again to Southwark by 2nd mo. 1769. In 1775 he moved back again with his wife and two children, and taught in the same school as had Jonah Thompson when he had arrived in Yatton in 1730 'to teach a schoole'.

In 1784 he moved to Sidcot and started a school there in the same house as did William Jenkins, and was apparently very successful. In June 1808 it was bought for the Quakers as an alternative to Ackworth School which was highly oversubscribed, and to provide a school nearer to home for the children of Friends in the West Country. This was to be a boarding school for both boys and girls. John Benwell's school was closed and he sold his house and the estate of about fourteen acres to the Committee for the sum of £1500. He and his wife Martha offered to act for a while as superintendents 'without any gratuity other than board and residence'. Their daughter Mary was paid sixteen guinees a year for her services as schoolmistress. The first General Meeting for Sidcot School was held at Sidcot Meeting House on the 15th July 1808 with twenty-eight representatives present from meetings in Bristol and Somerset, Devonshire, Gloucestershire and Wiltshire Quarterly Meetings. The new school opened at the beginning of September 1808 with just nine pupils (six boys and three girls), but within a year the number of scholars was up to 32. John and Martha Benwell ran the new establishment in an honorary capacity for two years and in 1810

General Meeting gratefully acknowledged their services.

The Benwells moved to Pensford (near Bristol) for a time, before returning to Oakridge. John's interest in the school was maintained and for some years he served on the Committee. He was also active in Sidcot Meeting and was clerk of Monthly Meeting for many years. His beautiful copperplate handwriting first appears in the Monthly Meeting minutes in 1780 when he took over from John Thomas. The Benwells moved once more from Oakridge, down the lane to Sidcot Farm, where John Benwell died in 1824. He was very much missed by everyone, especially his old scholars. He was 'obeyed because beloved', as the relative of one old scholar put it.

The Sidcot Ghost

No history of Sidcot Meeting would be complete without the story of the Sidcot ghost, or poltergeist. Whether it was due to some supernatural agency or to trickery has never been discovered, although the scene was visited by various people including Hannah More, the well known local philanthropist, who found no sign of trickery.

There was once a cottage which was situated across the lane from the Meeting House in Harbury Batch, standing approximately where Fairview now stands. In it lived a man who had quite a reputation in the neighbourhood, not only as a cattle-doctor, but also as a conjurer. Tradition even credits him with wearing a red cap and possessing a wizard's staff and magic books. When the time came for him to die he asked to be buried under a tree in the garden; some versions even have him wanting to be buried at the local crossroads so that he might watch the passers by. His words to his wife were (according to tradition) "If 'ee don't, I'll trouble 'ee". His demands were not met, however, and on the 27th July 1788, he was buried in Winscombe churchyard.

A year went by. Friends were sitting in their usual midweek meeting for worship, when the silence was broken by the entrance of the woman who took care of the meeting house and lodged with the widow. The woman seemed terrified and cried: "Oh Friends, do 'e come! Here be all Widow Beacham's things a'vallen about the vloor!" Two Friends, John Benwell and Charles Strode, got up and left the room, probably thinking of preventing further disturbance of the meeting. When they entered the door of the cottage the sight that met their eyes was apparently that of chairs and tables, pots and pans dancing about the room, and Joan's heavy kneading-trough (which she used to make cakes to sell) was rocking as if moved by invisible hands. The disturbance continued long enough to be witnessed by other Friends who came across to the cottage after meeting had ended. Among them was John Benwell's daughter Hannah (then aged about 12). Long afterwards she used to tell how, as she entered the cottage kitchen, she had to avoid a large and heavy armchair that was moving slowly across the room. Joan Beacham lived for another five years, but the disturbances did not recur and no one could unravel the mystery.

QUAKERS AT SIDCOT

The Chest

The chest in which Friends used to keep all the documents was first kept by Abraham Thomas, and then by his son, John Thomas. Over the years it must have got very full and untidy in spite of being sorted out occasionally. In 1784 it was John Hipsley's and Edward Gregory's turn to sort it and several Trust deeds appeared to be missing. The books and pamphlets were put in order and those which were suitable for handing around were bound in three volumes. Others were tied in parcels, numbered and were put in a chest which John Hipsley kept in Congresbury. He was to be in charge of books for the future. However, John Thomas was still in charge of the chest which contained the certificates and Trust deeds. John Benwell was asked to write a catalogue of books in the back of the Monthly Meeting minute book, which was very neatly done.

In 1802, when John Thomas died the chest was passed on to his nephew Thomas Tanner, and when John Hipsley moved away care of the books seems to have passed to John Benwell and Edward Gregory. In 1805 Edward Gregory of Yatton found room in his house for a repository for the deeds etc., and Thomas Tanner was discharged of his duties.

In 1896 the safe was moved from Yatton to Weston-super-Mare (which had a Meeting House by that time) and Charles Brown was appointed 'Keeper of the Records'.

Books

Ever since 1694 when William Lawrence had received a copy of George Fox's journal 'for theyer use and service from tyme to tyme...' Friends had been on the look out for suitable books. In 1697, William Lawrence was paid 3s.6d for 'bookes on Friends account'. At the same Monthly Meeting in 1697 it was stated: 'Itt is the sence and conclusion of Friends of this meeting that what Friends bookes is in any Friends hands that belong to this monthly meeting, the said Friends do bring them in to this meeting for the further use of Friends and truth, or else pay for them to the stock, that they may not live dormant in private Friends hands.' In other words, 'bring the books back or else pay for them'! At Quarterly Meeting in 1st mo. 1700 Northern Monthly Meeting ordered 98 copies of Robert Barclay's Apology!

In 1714 the Monthly Meeting ordered 42 of Thomas Ellwood's books, and Sidcot paid £1.10s for ten. Sidcot Meeting also ordered nine of John Whiting's books in the following year, fifty were ordered altogether by Monthly Meeting. In 1720 the Monthly Meeting was asked how many copies would be required of the translation of the 'History of the Christian People called Quakers' written in Dutch by William Sewell. William Jenkins was the only one from our Monthly Meeting area to want one. There is still a copy (not the same one) in the library.

A history of the life of Thomas Story was given to Friends by the author in 1748, and Sidcot received one copy, as they did in 1755 in the case of Benjamin

INTO THE EIGHTEENTH CENTURY

Holmes' journal. In 1756 John Thomas brought two copies of 'The Life and Travels of Samuel Bownas deceased', and in 1792 Joseph Naish and John Benwell received from the Meeting for Sufferings the following books:

2	Robert Barclay's *Apology*	
2	Wm. Penn's *No Cross, no Crown*	
2	Anthony Pearson on Tythes	
6	Wm. Penn's *Primitive Christianity*	
6	Wm. Penn's *Rise and Progress*	
24	*Summary of Our Principles.*	

These were left with Joseph Naish and John Benwell to distribute 'at their discretion'. This reading list must have kept Friends busy for a while.

By 6th mo. 1821 things were getting more organised. Particular meetings were asked to update their catalogues and to consider additions, as well as the best method of publicising the collection and 'ready access to all who may wish to peruse the books'. In 2nd mo. 1822 the Monthly Meeting was concerned that not enough people were getting access to their books. It was suggested that a catalogue should be made of that meeting's limited stock, which should be forwarded to each particular meeting, hoping that 'will produce the effects desired more compleatly than adding to our almost dormant Stock of Books'. Libarians today will recognise the difficulties, especially the problem of publicising the collection. Sidcot Meeting itself had no proper library until 1906, when William and Mary Miller donated a collection of books.

Money

Timothy Willis' will which was to be disposed of 'to the poor of the people called Quakers' is typical of the wills at the turn of century. On the 27th of 11th mo. 1698 he left £5 to be distributed as the Monthly Meeting thought fit. They did it as follows:

To William Watts of Nemnett by Wm. Reeve	£1.00s.00d
To Thomas Bean by John Dando	£1.00s.00d
To William Watts of Nemnett by Wm. Reeve	£1.00s.00d
To Thomas Bean by John Dando	£1.00s.00d
To Thomas Rose of Froome by Charles Rogers	5s.00d
To the widow Jennings of Banwell by Wm. Reeve	10s.00d
To Thomas Winscomb by John Hipsley	5s.00d
To the widow Mary Ram of Yeaton by Jo Allen	5s.00d
To John Brodway of Clareham by Rich. Thomas	5s.00d
To Richard Nethin of Ken by John Whiting	5s.00d
To Robert Line of Nemnet by John Whiting	5s.00d
Towards the binding of Walter Ismead his son Charles to John Tylee by Rich. Marchant	£1.00s.00d

QUAKERS AT SIDCOT

The previous month the will of William Lawrence had been shared out. He had left £2, and apart from Mary Jennings and Robert Lyne who each received 5s, it all went to different people.

Apart from wills, the General Stock was the main source of income for looking after the poor. At Bath 7th 3rd mo. 1716 the collections were as follows:

Portishead Mtg.	£1.19s.00d
Chew Mtg.	£1.03s.00d
Beluton Mtg.	14s.00d
Frome Mtg.	£1.11s.06d
Hallatrow Mtg.	10s.00d
Sidcot	£3.05s.06d
Bath & Bathford	£3.18s.00d
Keynsham	£3.01s.06d
Claverham	£4.00s.06d
	£20.03s.00d

With the decline in meetings there was much less donated, for instance 1st mo. 1751:

Portishead Mtg.	£0.14s.6d
Claverham Mtg.	£2.04s.0d
Sidcot Mtg.	£1.02s.6d
Chew (double coll.)	10s.0d
Keynsham "	10s.0d
Bath	£2.18s.6d
	£7.19s.6d

A collection was made as found necessary, and when it was considered too little by Quarterly Meeting it was sent back 'with desires that friends would consider the necessity that there is for a more liberall Collection...'. This happened in 1722 when the Monthly Meeting almost doubled its collection, from £6.8s.6d to £12.13s.0d.

At Quarterly Meeting on the 18th of the 4th mo. 1719 a proposition was put about starting a half year meeting for organising bequests to the poor, apprenticeships etc.. By 22nd 10th mo. 1720 it had been held, Abraham Thomas attending, to 'general satisfaction.' It must have continued to be generally satisfactory, at least until around 1790 when a Committee of Charities was set up to take its place.

Another collection was for the National Stock, which was a regular annual collection for national usage. Sidcot Meeting gave around £2.2s for many years.

INTO THE EIGHTEENTH CENTURY

There was also an annual collection for Ackworth School, then, when Sidcot School was founded, it was substituted by one for Sidcot.

In 1793 there was the first sign that Sidcot Friends were beginning to look at social concerns which went beyond needy members of the Society. A Committee was appointed to 'make application to friends in easy circumstances....for Subscriptions towards erecting a house in Yorkshire for the Accommodation of Lunatics' (the Retreat). Among the subscriptions were £1.1s from John Thomas, and £1.11.6. each from William Tanner and Thos. Tanner, from a total of £28.7s. The Retreat was built by William Tuke of York and became a model in the treatment of the insane. There is another indirect association with Sidcot. In 1804 John Hipsley (grandson of Richard and Ann, and son of John and Elizabeth, who moved to Ackworth) married Mabel Tuke, and became very much associated with the Tuke family. He supported them in their many philanthropic endeavours; he was interested in education and helped to set up a School at Rawden for children who were not members of the Society; and was actively supportive of the abolition of the slave trade. He and his wife were married for nearly sixty years, and he died peacefully at Hull in 1866 at the age of ninety one.

Another well-intentioned Subscription which seems more controversial in retrospect was that in 1806 'to assist friends in America in the civilization of the Indian natives....' This amounted to £82.13s.6d., of which £8.3s.6d. was from persons outside the society.

Apart from the routine distribution and collection of money one comes across some snippets which show a little of what life must have been like for eighteenth century Quakers. For example in 1712: '...sent Wm. Cray as token of friends Love to him in his illness .....10s by John Lovell'.

In 1721: '...to Joseph Manning for the rebuilding of some part of his dwelling house which was fell down.....£1.10s by Abraham Thomas'.

In 1723: 'Paid to Abraham Thomas for house rent for Henry Stone two pounds and to John Jenkins for a shroud for sd. Henry seaven shillings'.

In 3rd. mo. 1724 a £5. legacy was received from '.....our ancient and worthy Friend John Whiteing of London'. (The John Whiting who had lived in Wrington and had moved to London, but who obviously had kept in touch with Friends in the district.)

In 3rd mo. 1727 (held at Richard Hipsley's house at Stock): 'Paid John Hipsley six pounds and ten shillings it being our Quota of Charges settled at our last Quarter Meeting relating to the Prosecution at the late assizes held at Taunton on a Person that was indited and found guilty of that Horrable murder commited on the body of Mary Cuffe a poor friend that lived in Belluton Meeting House'.

In 1st mo. 1742 we read that 'John Thomas have paid his Unkle Arther £3.12.6 for the Surgeons Attendance of Clement Warly Deceased....' John Thomas's 'Unkle Arther' was Arthur Thomas of Cleeve.

In 1745: 'The manuscript book of Advice is brought here by Richard Marchant, who have also a pair of Leather Baggs to carry that and the Monthly Meeting book....' John Corbyn was paid 11s by John Thomas from the General Stock for getting them made. [N.B. The change of date 1751 52. After December 1751, January was called the 1st mo., February the 2nd mo. etc.. Previous to this the year had started in March.]

In 1782 we read that Widow Willmott was not able to provide anything for her children, so £16.16s was provided for a year's board for two of them. They had 8s.8d for pocket money, and 4d for postage of a letter. They had received £8.8s from 1/2yrs meeting and the balance of £8.17.0 was paid by the cashier from the General Stock.

On 1st of the 1st mo. 1787 at Claverham we learn that William Paine, who was meant to go to Ackworth School had died. £6.2.9 had been forwarded for clothing and sundry expenses, and an allowance for travel of 2d per mile for 179 miles, £1.9.10..

In 1st mo. 1837 it was agreed to pay the coach fare from Sidcot to Exeter, which amounted to £2, for two Friends travelling in the ministry, and agreed to pay all such expences in future.

As can be seen from the above, there was very little inflation during the eighteenth century. The cashier's accounts for the year 1794 can be seen below:

From the Monthly Meeting Accounts 1794

THE NEW MEETING HOUSE, 1817

In 4th. mo. 1811 Sidcot Preparative Meeting felt their Meeting House needed enlarging as there was not room for Sidcot School General Meeting, nor when a public meeting was held. They took a plan to Quarterly Meeting, and they appointed a joint committee to look into things. I think it is worth quoting the findings of that committee in full as it gives the best picture we possess of the old Meeting House on Harbury Batch.

Sidcot 22nd of 7th mo. 1811
We the undersigned met according to the appointment of the Quarterly Meeting and upon examination we find the Meeting house at this place is sufficiently large to accommodate the friends who usually attend Meetings for Worship, and nearly the whole of the Children of both the Schools, without making use of the Gallery, and that with the addition of fitting up the Gallery with proper seats, it may be made to accommodate them at their Monthly Meetings also, and when a small alteration is made in the manner of placing the seats and removing the front Door it will be sufficient for all purposes, excepting for large public Meetings.

Committee of Q. Meeting   John Thomas   Rchd. Ball
Jas. Torvill   Benjn. Fryer
Ditto of Monthly Meeting   Robt. Gregory   Edmd. Naish
Wm. Norris

This was obviously not very satisfactory for the school who wanted a bigger Meeting House, so in 1816 the General Meeting provided a plot for that purpose. The old Meeting House was to be sold for £80 to Peter Welsh, a cordwainer and a Friend who had recently been accepted into membership. The Burial Ground, was looked after by Harriet Welsh. Eventually a stone was set in the wall of the burial ground saying "FRIENDS' BURIAL GROUND 1690". It is still there.

A.T.Tanner was given the job of collecting subscriptions, and to these were added the proceeds from the sale of Hallatrow Meeting House which was £60, Axbridge Burial Ground £24, and Wm. Jenkins' plot which was sold to Charles Strode for £20. The total amounted to £1,228.11.6d!

This seems rather a lot to pay for what was considered by some to be 'a barn of a place'. There was no lobby, no cloakrooms, and almost no ventilation, and the whole place was lit by candles. (I should think this would be a good subject for the Drowsiness Committee!) There was ample stabling, however, where the small meeting room now stands, and there was a caretaker's house. Two hedges of hornbeam led up straight to within a few metres of the door of the Meeting House. On the right hand side were the boy's gardens and on the left a paddock, both surrounded by hedges. There were no buildings on the other side of the road at that time.

Sidcot Meeting House in 1817 ... 'a barn of a place'

No ghostly legend is connected with the new Meeting house. However, Francis Knight tells the story of Lavington Parmiter. About the year 1833, Lavington Parmiter was sitting in Meeting one Sunday, when he had a presentiment that all was not well at home. He left before the rest of the Friends dispersed, and hurried down to his shop in Winscombe. There, sure enough, he surprised a burglar in the very act of ransacking the shop. The robber was caught, tried, convicted and transported to Tasmania.

Weston-Super-Mare Meeting House, and Fire Insurance
In the 7th mo. 1844 Thomas Follett reported that Richard Parsley had offered a site in Weston-super-Mare for a Meeting House 'if friends be disposed to accept it '. A committee of friends was appointed to look into the matter. At the same meeting friends were appointed to consider 'insuring all or any of our Meeting Houses against loss by fire' and report.

The friends asked to report on the proposed Meeting House at Weston-super-Mare stated that 'for many years during the summer season a meeting for worship has been held in private apartments, by visitors attending that place and also by the few members of this Monthly Meeting from time to time resident there'. They also reported that since the opening of the railway (in 1843) the number of visitors coming 'for the purpose of Sea Bathing' was increased. Added to this the site was in a good position, and the committee definitely

THE NEW MEETING HOUSE 1817

recommended the acceptance of the offer. So the idea was put to Quarterly Meeting, and there it was decided to accept Richard Parsley's offer. The committee was desired to accept subscriptions.

Weston-super-Mare Meeting House was ready for use by 9th of 9mo. 1846, and Quarterly Meeting agreed to the holding of meetings there. Thomas Follet was asked to procure the necessary licence, but it was 'intended that Friends at Weston shall for the present continue under the Sidcot Meeting'.

Meanwhile, it had been decided to insure all the Meeting Houses in case of fire, and this gives an idea of the relative value of them all. Sidcot Meeting House was insured for £500, Bath for £400, Chew Magna for £100, Claverham for £200 and Portishead for £150.

The Fire of 1858

In spite of the insurance, when the Meeting House did catch fire the Insurance Money only amounted to £25.17s .9d., and Sidcot Meeting had to have a subscription to raise money for the repairs.

I quote from Francis Knight's 'History of Sidcot School'. He had found an Old Scholar of the school who remembered the occasion: '"We were sitting in the school-room one Wednesday morning, all ready to go into Meeting. But time passed. The old clock in the classroom struck eleven, and still there was no order to march. At length one of the teachers announced that the Meeting-house was on fire, adding the exciting news that we must help to put it out. I was one of a line of boys from the swimming-bath, through the shed-door, to the Meeting-house, and we passed buckets of water from hand to hand, and up to

Francis Knight in 1908 — from the Old Scholars' Report of that year

the masters and bigger boys, who, mounted on ladders, tore the slates off the roof, and threw water amongst the blazing rafters, which by this time were sending up a prodigious column of smoke. The fire was put out at last, but a great deal of damage had been done, and the building was not used for some weeks. We had Meeting in the girls' school-room for a long time, which, together with the fact that we all got soaked from head to foot, in passing the buckets of water, is what I remember most about the whole affair"'.

The Seaman Family

Samuel Hipsley Seaman was descended from the Hipsley family who lived in Shiplet. He married contrary to the rules in 1805 and 'did not appear to be so sensibly affected with a sense of his deviations as could be wished...', so he was disowned. He was reinstated ten years later, and his wife and large family followed a year after that. He was a regular representative at Monthly Meetings.

The first of Samuel Seaman's children to get into trouble was Robert, who was disowned in 1836, for not attending meetings. At the same time Albert Seaman was accused of being 'guilty of drinking to excess, profane swearing and other disorderly conduct,' so he was disowned too. In 1841 Samuel Seaman jnr. was disowned for dishonest and unchristian conduct but he appealed to Quarterly Meeting and won his appeal, so the Monthly Meeting decision was annulled. Meawhile Abraham and Eliza Seaman wanted to resign. Abraham's resignation was accepted after one visit, but Eliza kept changing her mind and in the end she decided not to resign, at her father's wish, but realized that she would be expected to attend meeting more often. This she obviously did until she was disowned for marrying out in 1860.

At the same Monthly Meeting which was considering Eliza's case (10/8/1842) Sidcot Friends reported that Samuel had been speaking in meeting for worship 'his communications having proved very painful and burdensome to friends'. He was visited twice and on the second occasion let drop a remark 'that he thought it probable he should have less to say in future', so Monthly Meeting decided to give him one more chance. Nevertheless, he was told he should make no further communications in meetings, which he refused to do; in fact Monthly Meeting was told by an overseer 'Samuel Seaman's communications have continued in every Meeting for Worship in which he has been present and that they have been of the same objectionable character'. They decided to disown him in 10th mo. 1842, but he again decided to appeal to Quarterly Meeting. However, this time he was not successful, and the appeal was rejected. One can't help wondering whether his 'objectionable' ministry stopped, however.

Daniel, William and Henry Seaman seemed very elusive when John Bishop and William Eddington were sent to visit them in 1847. Only William was in the first time they called at Shiplate, and he did not give them much hope that he and his brothers would attend Meeting more regularly. The visitors sent a letter the next time but 'on getting there we found them from home and had left word

THE NEW MEETING HOUSE 1817

with their Father that they had other engagements elsewhere.' Monthly Meeting 'under the conviction that no further labour will be to any avail' decided to disown them.

Samuel Hipsley Seaman died 3/9/1856 having seen most of his family either resign or be disowned.

The Tanner Family

For more than a hundred years of the history of Sidcot Meeting, members of the Tanner family were in evidence. William Tanner of Thornbury, Gloucester, proposed intention of marriage in 8th mo. 1720, with Rachel Thomas, sister of John Thomas, daughter of Abraham and Grace. They were married at Sidcot on 19/9/1740, and immediately moved away. They moved back into the area from Frenchay in 11th mo. 1761, and William soon got down to his Monthly Meeting duties.

William Tanner Jnr. was also on the list of those present at Monthly Meeting for Sidcot in the 12th mo. 1762. He married Hannah Curtis in 1771. Rachel's other children were Mary, John and Thomas. Mary married Edward Horwood of Bristol in Sidcot Meeting 21/10/1770. John married Hannah Player of Nailsea 13/4/1774, where they presumably lived for a while before they eventually moved to Portishead. There they both became valued members of Portishead Meeting. Thomas married Sarah Bishop at Belluton on 23/6/1779. He remained in the Sidcot area but always had to be distinguished from the other Thomas Tanner who lived at Winthill.

Rachel died before any of her children were married, and William married again in 1775, to Hannah Vowles of Portishead. Hannah outlived her husband for many years and became regular at the women's Monthly Meeting, and an overseer. Her children were Mary, Rachel and Arthur Thomas.

Arthur Thomas Tanner married Mary Gregory in 1814, and he was appointed to be Monthly Meeting Clerk in 1818, taking over from John Benwell. Mary did much visiting in the neighbourhood, and held public meetings, in which she was eventually accompanied by her son William. Mary Tanner became one of the best known figures in Sidcot Meeting, and her gentle and appealing ministry in worship was a noteworthy feature of Sidcot life. In 1831 Mary Tanner was accepted as a minister, and it was not long before she was travelling in the ministry, sometimes with her sister Elizabeth Gregory, sometimes with her husband, sometimes alone, and eventually with her son, William, who was appointed as a minister in 1839. They mainly travelled locally in Cheddar, Axbridge, Shipham, Banwell etc., but they did manage a trip to Ireland to Dublin Yearly Meeting, in 1842, and another in 1859. Monthly Meeting had a sort of formula for the minutes for people who were about to travel in the ministry, and another for people returning them. Women friends were always present on such occasions. For example, 10th of 9th mo. 1834:

QUAKERS AT SIDCOT

Our friend Mary Tanner, having in a feeling manner, informed this meeting that she believes to be required of her to hold a public meeting with her neighbours in this place; and many friends having expressed much unity and sympathy with in her apprehended religious duty, this meeting fully unites therewith and sets her at liberty for that service.

When she returned the minute, she explained that the Public Meeting had been held and that 'she has thankfully acknowledged that she was enabled to relieve her mind of the burden that had rested upon it so as to be productive of peace.' The actual words varied, but their meaning was always the same; then the women left.

William Tanner took great interest in the people of Cheddar where he was a paper manufacturer. He was a friend of William Barnes, the Dorset poet, and he enjoyed giving readings in dialect, the Dorset dialect being very similar to that of Somerset. He was also a friend of Hannah More and her sister, and took pleasure in following up her work in the district, setting up schools for poor children. He was very popular at Sidcot School too, being an expert on local Geology and Botany. It is said that he measured the height of Cheddar Cliffs by the simple means of lying full out on the highest point and lowering a plummet into the gorge below. I find this difficult to believe, but one must remember that there were very few trees in Cheddar Gorge at that time.

William was married, in 1849, to Sarah Wheeler, the daughter of Daniel Wheeler, and soon afterwards he and his wife moved to Bristol. (Daniel Wheeler was famed for his work in draining the marshes of St. Petersburgh, and Sarah had lived in Russia for about 10 years, from the age of 11). While in Bristol he gave 'Three Lectures on the Early History of the Society of Friends in Bristol and Somersetshire' which were published in 1858, and of which there is presently a copy in the library at Sidcot Meeting. He died on the 8th of the 11th mo. 1866, aged 51, after a short illness, watched over by his brother Arthur, sister Margaret, mother and invalid wife.

There was a great Great Meteor Shower on 13th November that year, which was watched from the roof by the pupils of the school. It was also seen by two men who were digging William Tanner's grave. He had died at his home at Ashley Hill in Bristol but was to be buried at Sidcot, where, although it was late, the men were still at work. They looked up into the sky and thought for a moment that it was the end of the world. They threw down their tools and ran. His wife died soon after, on the 1st of the 4th month 1867, aged 60, and was also buried at Sidcot.

Arthur Thomas Tanner died on 16/9/58. He had been very involved with the building of the new Meeting House in 1817, and had been given the job of collecting the subscriptions. He was a good Monthly Meeting Friend, described in the minute given him to take to Ireland as 'an elder in good standing amongst us.'

Mary Tanner died in 1869, causing great sadness at Sidcot, and elsewhere. At Yearly Meeting in 1869 John Hodgkin described her simple faith. About 35 years previously, when there was some trouble at Yearly Meeting, she went to London and obtained permission to visit the Men's meeting. She was able in a rather remarkable way to pour oil on troubled waters. There were other testimonies to her patience, cheerfulness, and large capacity for sympathy with the officers of Sidcot School. Many an Old Scholar remembered her with affection, as she sat at the head of the meeting dressed in modest Quaker dress, and rose to minister in her gentle voice.

Arthur Tanner of Oakridge was much missed when he died in 1866. He was very interested in natural history, and his collection of birds, as Francis Knight says, 'shot and stuffed by himself', were presented to the School by his widow, Margaret Tanner, who survived him thirty-five years. Francis Knight tells the story of how a large flock of crossbills, fairly uncommon birds, once appeared in the trees behind Oakridge House. But it was Sunday morning, and Arthur Tanner had a tussle with his Conscience. Which was better, to capture the birds or to honour the Sabbath? The Sabbath won, the birds were left in peace, and next morning the birds had flown, and never again visited the Oakridge fir trees. So much for the idea of every day being of equal importance! And so much for conservation!

Margaret Tanner, wife of Arthur, had previously been married to Daniel Wheeler (son of the Daniel Wheeler of St. Petersburgh fame), and she was a great campaigner. She helped Josephine Butler in her moral campaigns, and spoke at meetings and helped women to be fully accepted as an integral part of Yearly Meeting. Nevertheless, when, in 1880, Henry Barron Smith was appointed Clerk to the Quarterly Meeting on Ministry and Oversight, and Margaret Tanner was appointed Assistant Clerk, she made very clear that she did not wish to be clerk in his absence. She hoped 'that a man may be appointed to take his place'!

Mary Anna Tanner was married, by a priest, to a certain Robert Clark. However, he was of 'an upright Christian character', and the ceremony was carried out in a dissenting church. She still wished to continue coming to meeting, so it was decided to let the matter rest. She lived in Combe House and was able to help the School Committee out when they had difficulties about a piano. They were in dead-lock over whether they could allow a piano in School, so Mary Anna Clark invited some of the girls into her home to meet a teacher on Saturday mornings, and some very enthusiastic lessons ensued.

More Deaths at Sidcot

In 1866 Abraham Tanner of Winthill died, aged 76, and it is said the country people lined the route from Banwell Castle to the Meeting House on their way to his funeral. William Higgins, aged 79, who became a regular occupant of the Minister's gallery, although he seldom spoke, died the following year. Thus

QUAKERS AT SIDCOT

Sidcot lost two overseers.

Tom Tanner of Winthill, died in 1869, aged 52. He sat behind the boys, and in the words of Francis Knight: 'If the Friends at the top of the Meeting were late in concluding, Tom Tanner would pull out his watch, extracting it from cavernous depths inside his waistcoat. After a brief interval he would put on his hat. If these hints were disregarded, he would impatiently scrape his feet along the floor - a proceeding which seldom failed to produce the effect he wanted. It was said that he had declared he would rather stand up to his neck in a horse-pond than read a book. Driving out of the Meeting-house yard one day, he overturned his gig against the guard-stone at the foot of one of the gate-posts; and although he got up and righted the carriage and drove home to Winthill, his knee was so severely injured that he died of lock-jaw (tetanus) a few days later.'

Edward Hallam, the Axbridge chemist died in 1867; Joseph Miles of Langford who had sat facing the Meeting for many years, and had been on numerous committees, died in 1875; his brother Edwin had died in 1864. Hannah Gregory, a cousin of William Tanner, aged 86, died at Sidcot 1/11/1866, and William Tanner mentioned, the day before he died, in a letter to a friend, his intention of going to Sidcot to his cousin's funeral. All these deaths led to a particularly low point in the meeting's history and apart from members of the school community there were very few members attending meeting.

The Alterations to the Meeting House

At Sidcot Preparative Meeting on 5th, of 12th mo. 1869, a Committee was appointed 'to consider whether any alterations or improvements' were necessary on the Meeting House premises. They were, and the plans were passed by both Monthly Meeting and Quarterly Meeting. The estimate for the improvements was about £360, but a further £80 would be required for doing the inside of the building.

In the 3rd month of 1872 the committee were ready to report:

To the Monthly Meeting:

We have pleasure in reporting that the work at Sidcot Meeting House is now completed. In accordance with the plans laid before the Monthly Meeting in the 4th mo. 1870, there have been erected a new Entrance Vestibule, Mens and Womens Cloak Rooms and Offices and a covered Passage Way and the alterations necessarily involved in the Caretaker's Cottage adjoining have been made. In addition to the primary uses of these erections the main building of the Meeting House is protected by them from the violent winds to which its situation exposes it, and the general appearance of the House is strikingly improved.

The repairs effected in the interior of the Meeting House including alterations of seats, colouring of walls, varnishing of woodwork and lighting with gas have added much to its comfort and cheerful appearance and we believe

Above and below: *Views of the Meeting House early this century*

to its usefulness.

A new boundary wall and Iron Railing have been put up and the narrow strip of ground lying between the yard and the road has with the permission of Sidcot School (vide minute 19 under date 27th 4th mo. 1870) been thrown into the yard. The 22 Iron Pillars supporting the boundary railing are the kind gift of Nicholas Sara of Falmouth.

We are also indebted to the liberality of the late Joseph Pease for the valuable Turret Clock with bell, fitted in position at his cost, and which we believe fully realises his intention of its serving as the TimeKeeper for the School and whole neighbourhood. ... *

Signed Joseph Miles, Theodore Compton, Josiah Evans
Dated 11th of the 3rd mo. 1872

* The rest of the minute expresses gratitude for the fact that all the expenses have been met and notes that one copy of the plans of the Meeting House has been deposited at Sidcot and another in the Monthly Meeting chest.

It may be worth noting that, at the time this was written, neither the science block, nor the part of the school immediately opposite the Meeting House were built and hence there was no protection from westerly winds.

Other Meeting Houses

In 11th mo. 1863 it was decided to build a new Meeting House in Yatton, in a central position to replace the one at Claverham, which was so remote. Quarterly Meeting was asked for permission to sell Claverham Meeting House but it was not allowed. In 1877, Yatton Friends asked permission (which was granted) to hold meetings for worship there monthly on Sunday afternoons 'to which persons in the neighbourhood may be invited'. When Monthly Meeting decided to sell the Meeting House in the 1930s, it was bought by Roger Clark of Street who then gave it back to the Quarterly Meeting. When Quarterly Meetings were changed to General Meetings, their property devolved back to Monthly Meetings. When the question of selling it was raised again in the early 1980s, it came into the hands of the Friends' Historical Society, and the William Allen Society. Working parties and workshops are held there. Now, since September 1988, there have again been monthly meetings for worship held there on Sunday afternoons, organised by the part-time Warden (Marjorie Mallik) encouraged by an attender from Claverham. The meetings have been very successful and well attended so far.

Chew Magna Meeting House was sold in 1860. It had not been used for some time, because there was only one 'aged Friend' remaining, and some Friends from Brislington came and met in his house. The sale of the Meeting House raised £110, with £2 for the old benches, and that was put towards the

THE NEW MEETING HOUSE 1817

cost of the new Meeting House at Yatton, the land for which cost £500. It was ready for use in February 1867; meeting for worship was held in the morning, and Josiah Evans, Sidcot School's headmaster, held a public meeting in the evening.

At Yearly Meeting in 1874 there was the suggestion that Social Meetings should be held for the Monthly Meeting. The first was held at Yatton and was thought to be a 'satisfactory occasion'. There were nearly 90 Friends present, and it was decided to hold another at Sidcot. It was suggested that the pamphlet 'The Church in its relation to the State' be read at it! These were obviously not what immediately springs to mind when one thinks of Social Gatherings these days, with tables laden with good food, and a cup of coffee in one's hand. They were probably more like a large Monthly Meeting discussion group. It was not until about 1906 that a Social Gathering was held for the Preparative Meeting, which was a little more like the ones we are used to, when they used to have a social tea, followed by a speaker. In 1911, Bevan Lean even showed slides (made from Mabel Lean's photos.) of his tour of Egypt.

Clevedon's Meeting House was opened in July 1868. It was described as being situated in a good central position, and easily able to accommodate 150 persons. The report in the 'British Friend' goes on to say: 'In the morning about 60 Friends were present, including a deputation from the North division of Somerset M.M.. By the direction of the said M.M., the public were invited to an evening meeting, when the house was crowded by a company of nearly 200 persons.' The article goes on to say 'the immediate vicinity abounds with beautiful drives and walks; in one direction for miles over high hills, on which the air is particlarly fine and pure. Having railway communication with all parts of the country, Clevedon offers many attractions as a residence for any Friends who may wish to combine cheerfulness with with a fine and healthy country situation.'

The Meeting House at Bath was sold in 1867. It was situated in Lower Borough Walls and fetched £650. Bath Friends bought the Bethesda Chapel, previously the Freemasons' Hall, in York Street, where they still worship.

It seems amazing that, just when numbers attending meeting were so low, the Friends built such large buildings. Apart from anything else they must have been difficult to heat. Yatton is now the Primary School, and Clevedon, in spite of its 'fine and healthy country situation', did not attract sufficient numbers of Friends to move into the area. Nevertheless, the meeting is growing, and is hard to imagine that, with all the new estates which have been built, there are not a few potential Quakers in the area.

Perhaps one of the reasons they built the Meeting Houses so big was that they expected to hold public meetings in them, with talks given by travelling Friends. For example, when Henry Dymond spoke at Spiceland (a Meeting with strong Sidcot connections) he sent the following report: 'At Spiceland, where the Friends' Meeting House is situated at a considerable distance from almost every human habitation, the concourse of persons was very great; not one half of whom could be accommodated within the walls of the building; but crowded about the open windows and were very still and attentive to the close of the meeting.' He goes on to say. 'At Bradninch the Baptist Chapel was kindly lent for the occasion. The minister had a platform erected for us under the pulpit; he assisted in seating the numerous company; then took a seat by my side; and at the close of the meeting entreated the audience to accept the words of exhortation that had been offered among them'. Friends also wanted extra room for Monthly Meetings and Quarterly Meetings etc. especially as men and women needed separate rooms for business meetings.

The Meeting house at Weston-super-Mare was bombed during the second world war and the area redeveloped. The new Meeting house now faces the High street.

New Boundaries
Wiltshire Monthly Meeting was suffering particularly badly from the decline in numbers, and it was suggested that they should join with the North Division. The North Division agreed, so the first Joint Meeting was held at Melksham on 12th of 7th mo. 1876.

Sidcot Preparative Meeting Minutes
The earliest minute books for Sidcot Preparative Meeting are small, hard backed note books for the years 1847-1875, and 1886-1904. Found with the minute books was a small green accounts book called "Sidcot Preparative Meeting Collecting Book", starting with subscriptions for 1845. There is also a loose piece of blue, lined writing paper with a list of members of Sidcot Meeting in 1870.

Friends used to hold Preparative Meeting only once every three months before Quarterly Meeting, when they used to answer the set queries, choose representatives for the following Monthly Meeting, and appoint someone to make collections. The minutes were signed 'John Frank, Clerk'. Arthur T. Tanner and Benjamin G. Gilkes were the first premises committee when they were appointed 'to have the care of the Meeting house and premises belonging to Friends, in this place'. Henry Lees took over the job of clerk on 6/3/1864, and as Treasurer in 10th mo. 1854.

In 1861 when Henry Dymond was standing in as clerk Friends got into a bit of a muddle. The queries were answered, and the clerk was desired to take them to Monthly Meeting. There then follow the answers with the words 'These should not have been entered here' written in the margin. Each meeting still had to answer the Queries, and then Monthly Meeting had the job of combining them to send to Quarterly Meeting (see Appendix IV for an earlier set of queries, some of which were the same as those answered here). Although the answers are rather vague, I think they are worth quoting:

THE NEW MEETING HOUSE 1817

To the first. Our Meetings for worship are regularly held and the time appointed is generally observed. There is a little deficiency on the attendance on first days, and more on other days of the week.

To the second. We believe Friends are frequent in reading the Holy Scriptures, and that those who have Children or others under their care encourage them in the practice of this religious duty.

To the third. We believe a care prevails amongst many of our members to maintain a religious life and conversation, consistent with our Christian profession, and to train up their Children or others under their care in accordance therewith.

To the fourth. We believe Friends are preserved in love one towards another and that a care prevails to avoid and discourage tale-bearing and detraction.

To the fifth. With a little exception, we believe Friends are faithful in bearing our Christian testimony against all ecclesiastical demands.

To the Sixth. We believe Friends are faithful in maintaining our Christian testimony against all war.

Then Henry Dymond went travelling in the ministry, and they forgot to hold the next Preparative Meeting altogether. The first minute for 8th 9th mo. 1861 reads 'We accidentally omitted to hold our usual meeting in 6th mo. last'. Then Josiah Evans took over the Clerkship, and everything was back to normal.

From 1863 men and women Friends were together for all or part of each meeting, and a Conference of men and women Friends was held. From 1872 onwards the men and women seem to be together every time. Nevertheless, the screen which separated the two parts of the Meeting House remained in position until 1892, when it was removed due to increased numbers. The School Committee offered to bear the bulk of the expense, so I should imagine that it was the School which was growing rather than the Meeting, which was still at a fairly low ebb.

In 4th mo. 1891, the condition of the stones in the burial ground caused some concern because of the shaling due to frost, making the inscriptions illegible. It was 'decided in future to use stones of plain marble with the name, age and date of death inscribed with sunken letters of lead, the size to be 24"x14"x3". Such stones can be supplied by John Bennett of Clevedon at a cost of 30s each on the ground'.

From 1902 the Minute Books look much more organized. Instead of answering a Query first, they start with the words, 'The minutes of last meeting have been read and signed', but at least one of the Queries was always read at the end of the meeting (until 1906, when it was decided that it would be better if it were read in meeting for worship). The minutes were signed by John Grubb, who was Clerk at the time.

QUAKERS AT SIDCOT

Charles Gilpin and William Tallack

Charles Gilpin was a scholar of the school (older brother of Joseph Sturge Gilpin who became a member of the Sidcot School staff), and was the only Old Scholar who became a member of the British Government. He first entered Parliament in 1857, and the most prominent feature of his career was his strenuous effort to abolish the death penalty. He was also a close friend of Lajos Kossuth, the exiled Hungarian leader of the 1848 revolution against the Hapsburgs, and tried to champion his cause.

William Tallack was also an ardent campaigner for the abolition of the death penalty. He had been an apprentice at the school, and was one of the few who had completed his full seven years, but when he left in 1852 for Pontefract, he left the teaching profession. In 1866 he founded the Howard Association (the Howard League, as it is known now) and was Secretary for more than thirty years. The Howard League works to prevent crime and tries to find the best way of treating prisoners. William Tallack was also Secretary of the Society for the Suppression of Capital Punishment, and addressed numerous meetings and wrote many letters and pamphlets on the subject. Public executions were still carried out at that time (1864), and there had been a recent one at Newgate, with full press coverage. Public executions continued until 1868.

There was a local public execution of three men at Kenn, near Yatton, in September 1830, which could not have escaped the notice of Friends. The men had been found guilty of setting fire to three stacks of wheat belonging to Benjamin Poole of Kenn, and the High Sheriff decided that they should be executed near the scene of the crime. They went via Axbridge, and presumably passed through Sidcot, or nearby. At Kenn the gallows had already been erected, and a huge crowd (about twelve to fourteen thousand according to the "Taunton Courier"!) had gathered to witness the spectacle. They were duly hanged, the youngest of them, Richard Clarke, being only eighteen years old.

The Franco-Prussian War and other concerns

On 9/10/1870 a minute from Meeting for Sufferings was read about the desirability of raising money for the Victims of the War raging on the Continent. A total of £78.6s.7d was sent to London, from Sidcot, which was quite a lot considering Friends were also collecting for the alterations to the Meeting House. Besides the money, the following contributions in seed were sent: 22 bags of potatoes, 6 bags of peas, 2 bags of spring wheat and 3 bags of barley. Clothing was also needed and the meeting was informed that some had been sent to the Depot in London. The black and red Quaker Star was introduced to identify these relief contributions, and was also displayed by the volunteers who went to the battlefields. It has often been used since, and was eventually adapted (by introducing the dove symbol) to be the logo of Quaker Peace & Service.

In 1872 Sidcot Friends were much concerned with the purchase of a new

THE NEW MEETING HOUSE 1817

stove for the Meeting House, but at the same time their thoughts were drawn further afield by the Yearly Meeting Epistle which was read after meeting, as it is now. I quote a part of it because the concerns expressed seem still very relevant today:-

> The present is a time of much apparent commercial prosperity. In the recollection of the many solemn warnings of the past, we would bid all beware of that spirit which "hasteth to be rich", and which so often leads those who give way to it, to trade beyond their ability, to the great hurt of themselves and their families, and to the grievous injury of others......
>
> We desire to encourage our Friends everywhere to use their influence to remove from the earth the blot of slavery wherever it exists: whether in eastern Africa, in Cuba, or in the Islands of the Pacific......
>
> Our attention has been again directed to the enormous evils attending the spirit and the practice of war. Is the world to learn nothing from the lessons of the past? Scarcely have two of the principal nations of Europe emerged from one of the most awful conflicts of modern times, than we see them again arming, in seeming preparation for fresh struggles. It distresses us to think that even in our highly favoured country, in the midst of profound peace, attempts should be made to increase our military establishments, and to promote a martial spirit among the masses of the people...... The soldier cannot become skilled in the art of destruction, armaments cannot be raised or kept together, battles cannot be fought, multitudes of men cannot be slaughtered and their souls hurried into eternity, upon Christian principles......

In the following years there was mention of such subjects as trouble in Ireland, Temperance, the Opium Trade, Adult Schools, vivisection, poverty and peace. Sidcot Meeting organized some Public Peace Lectures in 1887, and in 1890 it was reported that the Adult School in the village was doing good work, averaging an attendance of 13. In 1900 a Minute was read from Monthly Meeting on the war in the Transvaal (the Boer War), but it was decided that nothing could be done apart from the private circulation of peace literature owing to the state of public opinion. In 1904, a Peace Deputation consisting of Edward Vipont Brown and his brother, William Brown, visited the School and Meeting. In the evening E. Vipont Brown gave a powerful address to a large public meeting.

In 1903 a committee was appointed to consider the systematic collection of subscriptions for Quaker work and outside concerns and to prepare a scheme. The scheme was approved at the following meeting, and William Miller and Elizabeth Chatfield were appointed collectors for the year.

QUAKERS AT SIDCOT

The Care of the Meeting House

The caretaker of the Meeting House, Maria Edwards, features in a reproduction of a photograph of the Meeting dating from about 1860. We read that in 1869, just before the alterations, the proposal from the Women's Preparatory Meeting was adopted that she should be paid £5 per annum. When James and Hannah Hemmens became caretakers in 1873, they were offered free rent and coals in addition to £5 per annum. The cost of the coals (about £4 15s a year) was eventually deemed to be excessive and the minutes of 11th 10mo 1874 record that after much consideration 'it is the judgement of this meeting that an allowance of £5 a year with free rent is an ample remuneration for the care of the premises'. It seems likely that the Hemmens disagreed because the meeting was soon looking for new caretakers.

On 7th 4th mo. 1872 Albert Fry and Josiah Evans were appointed to consider buying a new stove for the Meeting House. Josiah Evans left to go to Ackworth in 1873, so nothing was done about it until 9th mo. 1874, when Edmund Ashby was asked to confer with Samuel Dawes of Clevedon about it.

MEETING HOUSE OF 1817 AND 'LITTLE MARIA' (CARETAKER), SHOWING UPPING STONE AND PATTERN RACK.
From photograph, too faded for reproduction, taken about 1860.

(Reproduced from A Sidcot Pageant *by Evelyn Roberts)*

THE NEW MEETING HOUSE 1817

The result of this conference was a new stove which cost £3! It was almost certainly the same stove that was causing trouble in 1903. Sidcot P.M. decided that the best way of heating the building would be by a system of hot water pipes, but this would be very expensive and they decided to ask Monthly Meeting if it would defray some of the cost. The plea was obviously unsuccessful, and the next suggestion was that the stove should be moved further down the room and that the flue should go straight up through the roof. This was approved immediately and work was to be begun at once, and finished by the next month. The stove lasted until 1905, when a new stove was purchased for £4.15s.8d.

Triennial Reports on the Life of the Meeting
Monthly Meeting minutes record brief summaries about the life of each meeting every three years. This practice appears to have started in 1st mo. 1882. The report was given in 1887 that:

> The meeting at Sidcot claims special interest from the presence of the School household numbering 140. There is one resident recorded minister and another so frequently attends in the mid week as to be as much in sympathy with the congregation as if he were a member of it. Many other Friends visit the meeting and the truths of the Gospel as held by the Society are fully and often attractively put before the young. An attachment to Friends is undoubtedly strengthened in many whilst they are at the school and some of the small number there, unconnected with us evidently come to share this attachment.
>
> Successful meetings on Peace, Temperance, Missions & other good causes have been appreciated by the scholars and neighbours from the country around. Two classes for young men and one for young women are conducted by Friends in this small meeting. Two of these classes are in connection with other Dissenting bodies - a public coffee tavern is maintained & much of the Temperance work in the villages is done or directed by Friends.

It is fairly certain that the recorded resident minister was Edmund Ashby, the school's superintendent, and the regular visitor was Henry Barron Smith who kept a school in Weston. The Temperance work continued. In 3rd mo. 1901 it was reported that 'Many Friends are actively interested in Temperence Work in the village where there are two energetic Bands of Hope in existence.' Birds the Bakers was a Temperance Hotel. The Preparative Meeting minutes for 19/11/1893 record another Triennial Report with a breakdown of the membership. 'Sidcot Meeting is composed of 182 individuals, 40 adult members, 7 regular attenders, and 135 children, of whom 20 have not been trained to our method of worship. Of the 40 adults, 15 are officers at the School and 5 non-resident members. Our responsibility also extends to several others who casually attend as visitors or neighbours, among them a party of poor children from a convalescent home.'

Edmund and Eliza Ashby and family

THIS CENTURY

The Library

In 1896 Sidcot Meeting had no library, although quite a few meetings in the area did, but Sidcot Friends were allowed to use the one at Sidcot School. The library at the Meeting House started with a gift of Friends' books from William and Mary Miller in 1906. A bookcase had to be bought, and R. Christie Burn and Jane Knight were appointed to look through the list to see if the books were all suitable. They were kept busy because several people wanted to donate books, including Elizabeth Giles, who donated a china cupboard as well as a set of bookshelves, which had belonged to her father, William Pumphrey. Some of the books were very old and a committee was appointed to have them valued. Margaret Burcham was the first librarian with E. Maria Bishop as assistant. Some of the first new books to be purchased were: Memoirs of J.S. Rowntree, Palestine Papers by J. Wilhelm Rowntree and the Oxford Edition of Whittier's Poems. By 1907 the 'social tea' followed by a lecture was quite a regular feature, and Alfred Neave Brayshaw (a Sidcot Old Scholar) came to give a lecture on some of the books in the library, which 'was much enjoyed'. In 1918 Herbert Hutchinson took the library in hand and opened it to the public, and was given £5 for the purchase of new books.

The library was well used in the 1950's. The librarian's report for 1950 gives a total of over 100 books borrowed; but the total for children's books was 299! The library has continued to grow through gifts and new books bought, and now the Treasurer allows about £50 a year to spend on books. It has moved at least three times, once during the alterations of 1925 and once when the children's room was altered; then it was moved to its present position when the alterations of 1985 were completed.

Lectures

Besides giving the lecture on books, A. Neave Brayshaw was also invited to give an address on the early days of North Somerset Monthly Meeting for the School Centenary in 1908. In fact, he was a regular and popular visitor. Other lectures included those on Betting and Gambling, in 1905, when P.H. Wicksteed M.A. gave two lectures on the subject, and he also spoke to the School on Sunday evening. Then, Percy Alden M.P. spoke on 'The Social Conditions in Denmark', and A. Langman on The Opium Traffic. This concern about the opium trade continued, and in 1913 the Clerk sent the following resolution to the Prime Minister, The Secretary of State for India, The Foreign Secretary and

Helen Neatby and Neave Brayshaw in 1934

three MPs including the local one: 'This meeting, believing that the growth and manufacture of opium in India for export to China, enforced by appeal to Treaties, is morally indefensible and a serious hindrance to the spread of Christianity in the East, urges upon His Majesty's Government that, without further delay, China be formally released from Treaty obligations to admit opium, and that the connexion of the Indian Government with the opium export trade be brought to an end. G. F. Spencer Smith, Clerk. 1.VI.1913.'

Bible Study was central to Friends' thinking, and Mary K. Emmott read her paper on this subject. As a result, several small circles, each with about six members, were established to meet weekly or fortnightly to discuss the reading they had done on selected subjects. The idea behind making the groups so small was so that everyone should be able to make a useful contribution. Also, once a month during the winter, various lectures were given on Biblical subjects,

THIS CENTURY

School General Meeting 1907

followed by a discussion.

In 1908 Percy Alden MP visited the School again and this time he gave a lecture on Housing. This was held in the Meeting House and was attended by about 80 people. As a result a member of the meeting (Edmund Ashby?) arranged to build three houses for workmen in Winscombe!

The First World War

A special Preparative Meeting was held on the 9th of 8th month 1914 'to consider the responsibilities of Sidcot in relation to the outbreak of European War'. It was felt that Friends should work with others 'as far as conscience permits' rather than form any organization of their own.

The National Union of Women's Suffrage Societies suspended all political activity in favour of Emergency work, and the Winscombe branch obtained permission to use the committee room for Sewing Meetings for the 'benefit of Sufferers from the industrial and economic dislocation' caused by the war.

The collection for the National Relief Fund amounted to £44.16s.5d, which was sent to Buckingham Palace. An appeal was also heard from the Emergency Committee for the assistance of Germans, Austrians and Hungarians who were suffering in this country. The outbreak of war had left many 'enemy aliens' stranded and destitute, far from home, and subject to persecution and even violence. There was also an appeal for clothing, especially for women and children, for Belgian Refugees in Holland. A group of Belgian refugees actually spent some time in Sidcot. At the Meeting on 3/1/1915 there is a minute which

77

states 'Leave is granted to the Belgian Refugees for the use of the Committee Room for their Meetings for Worship on Sundays.' Then in a different writing underneath, 'The meeting for worship takes the form of Mass'. The Belgians left a lovely avenue of beech trees for the School when they left. Called Belgian Avenue, it leads from about half way up Fountain Lane across the field to Combe House. Sadly, many of the trees died after the long, hot summer of 1976 as a result of beech bark disease.

The Friends War Victims Relief Committee was revived and well supported by Sidcot Friends. Sidcot Friends were very upset by the attitude of Meeting for Sufferings which refused to recognise or acknowledge the work done by the young men who had joined the Friends Ambulance Unit, and Bevan Lean wrote a minute to that effect to be sent to the Clerk of Meeting for Sufferings. The attitude of the Society of Friends was that joining the F.A.U. was a matter of individual conscience. Corder Catchpool, an Old Scholar of Sidcot School was one of the founder members of the F.A.U., but when he discovered that he was given automatic exemption from conscription as a member of the F.A.U., he came home to face the tribunal. He served several terms of arduous imprisonment. Others felt that they were doing such useful work that they could never consider leaving.

Perhaps Sidcot School was less affected by the war than non-Quaker Schools, as few of the masters left for military service. However, they could not help being somewhat affected; some lost fathers or brothers, and they could not escape the shortage of food, or rationing. The older boys, with the support of Bevan Lean (the Headmaster) and the Preparative Meeting formed a Service Corps to tend the gardens of the elderly who could not cope, and to help the farmers. About twenty boys were involved, all over sixteen, and they missed some games days and put in two and a half hours on alternate Saturdays. They charged threepence an hour, which was waived in appropriate cases, and all money earned went to charity. The girls did fruit picking, light gardening and household tasks within the School. These activities finished soon after the war.

On 4/5/1919 it was reported that since the beginning of the war the following sums had been forwarded 'through the P.M.' (in addition to that sent by individuals): War Victims £943.13s.6d, Emergency Committee £332.10s, F.A.U. £393.11s.6d.. About 3500 garments were made in the sewing meetings. Sidcot School sent about £100 and many garments made in their leisure time. The minute ends with the words: 'We recognise how small is the help we have been able to give in comparison with the vast need, which must continue for a considerable time'.

The New School Hall
The lack of a school hall was felt severely at the beginning of the 1920's, the girl's playroom being inadequate, especially for the production of plays, but the Committee that was set up to examine the subject could come to no conclusions

and abandoned the idea for a year. The plan was to enlarge the Meeting which needed doing anyway, to make it suitable for a School Hall, but ther many difficulties: drama and music in the Meeting House for instance! 1 was one particular Clevedon Friend who went regularly to Monthly Meeti who just could not countenance dramatic performances in the building. At la there was one Monthly Meeting which she did not attend owing to illness, and the decision was made. She lived for many years after, but never again set foot in Sidcot meeting. The plan was eventually approved by the Committee and Staff of the School, and the Preparative Meeting agreed to it. The School Committee offered £1000 towards the extension, £500 was raised from the sale of Yatton Meeting House, and an appeal was launched for the rest (about £2000), mainly obtained from Old Scholars. The Friends were to retain the right to use it for all their usual purposes, but it was to be 'The School Hall', although the School undertook to see that there would be no dancing there.

Inside the Meeting House before the alterations —
The Old Scholars Exhibition, 1908

While the work was in progress, Friends met in Bird's Assembly Rooms (now the carpet showroom in the village), free of charge, and the Preparative Meeting wrote to express its appreciation for 'the kind help given' by Bird and Sons. In fact, some members preferred meeting in the centre of the village in spite of street noise and a gramophone playing in the background, and more people attended their meetings, particularly in the evenings, than would do so normally.

The new hall was first in use in March 1926, but there were teething

Photos] [P. Carpenter, May and July, 1925

"1925. THE PHOENIX."

Rebuilding the Meeting House as an enlarged School Hall

Cross-sectional plan drawing of Meeting House, 1925

troubles. A large piece of plaster fell on Miss Cameron during Band practice. A builder was called in and it was decided to take the loose sections down immediately, and Bevan Lean took a piece of plaster for his scholars to analyse in a chemistry lesson. The new plaster was not up in time for the Old Scholars Easter Reunion, but they seemed to have a good time, 170 old scholars signing the Register. There were ten big gatherings in five days in the new hall, culminating in the School's performance of 'St. Joan'.

When the accounts were finally presented in 1927 it was found that not only were the building costs met, but the Hall Committee had managed to provide a new grand piano and a cinema lantern, (presented by the O.S.) and paid for curtains and stage lighting. Many thanks were due to Eustace H. Clothier, an experienced business man, an O.S. who had come from Cardiff and settled in a house near the playing field. He was thorough and persistent and carried negotiations right through until completion. Bevan Lean worked hard too, writing to all parents and O.S. at least twice.

The Caretaker's cottage was in a bad state, too, and it was decided (in 1925) to build the bungalow in Oakridge Lane next to the Meeting House, and use the extra room for the library etc.. (The 'no coal' policy had been abandoned in 1919 when Mrs. Holt took over as Caretaker. She had a written agreement allowing her 10s/week, as well as free cottage and coal for the kitchen fire. She was provided with all cleaning materials and paid extra for washing up, 2s for 50 people, 2s.6d if over that number). The caretaker from 1925 onward was to be an employee of the School.

QUAKERS AT SIDCOT

REMINISCENCES

From Margaret E. Lloyd

In 1917 when I was at the School in the Upper Third Form, there was a celebration of the centenary of the Meeting house as it then existed. The Meeting and School together produced a version of Violet Hodgkin's 'Fierce Feathers'. Edmund Ashby, former Headmaster, who was always a kindly beneficent figure at the head of the Meeting, took the part of Zebulun Hoxie. Some of the older boys became a band of Indians, who ran round the Meeting house singing a war chant composed by Frederick Goudge the music master: I remember the words still.

Another person who remembers the 'centenary' well is Margaret Stone (nee Wedmore). She also remembers Samuel Wedmore (lived 1839 to 1920) who regularly drove over from Portishead to attend Sunday morning Meetings.

Margaret Lloyd also recalls Madeline Grubb, an Elder much concerned with the School and Meeting, who arranged a meeting with the Elders and sixth formers at her house, The Down, in the Avenue, perhaps the first of its kind. The Down was also the scene of many other meetings, including mid-week meetings for Elders and Overseers. It was also the scene of an enjoyable 'Congregational Gathering' in September 1919, at the invitation of John and Madeline Grubb. Over seventy attended, and after tea they played games in the garden.

Kenneth Southall (at school 1908-1911) remembers that

Dr. Lean gave the most wonderful scientific lectures, about once a year, in the Meeting house, and on one occasion he scattered minor explosives up the centre gangway. However, these did not all go off on Saturday night and Daddy B. (Christie Burn) set some of them off on Sunday, causing much amusement.

On Saturday night we had some sort of entertainment now and then, and apart from Dr. Lean's lectures the only other one I remember was when Jack Hoyland (I think it was him) recited the Jabberwocky and at the end of the last verse he fell flat on his face on the floor (the benches having been removed for that purpose). It was very exciting.

It might be of interest that when I first went to Sidcot I wore an Eton suit with starched white cuffs and a white front on Sundays. What a contrast with today! In the fourth form we were promoted to square cut black jackets; a great boost to morale.

Arthur Marsden (at school 1913-1916) told me the story of 'Old Man' Bobbett with the boots which he used to take off at the beginning of Meeting. The boys were not able see the clock from where they were sitting but they could see 'Old Man' Bobbett who was sitting opposite them. Every Sunday he put on

GROUP TAKEN AT THE MEETING HOUSE CENTENARY.

Below: *John and Madeline Grubb*

his boots at 11.55 am. so they could tell when meeting was about to end.

John Crowley was at the School from 1919-1925 and writes:

> The Winscombe postmaster at that time was Howard Brooks, a member of the Meeting, a dear man, self effacing and kindly. The Post Office was in his house with a little telephone exchange in an inner room. Once every term on a Sunday he and his sister Katie Brooks invited me and a companion to tea. There were always scones and jam and one of Birds' lovely cakes with white icing and walnuts on top. Howard would have to leave the tea-table from time to time to operate the telephone switchboard. Behind the post office house he had a small orchard and a press for making his own cider. I do not think he ever spoke in meeting but I always knew if he was there.
>
> One very hot Sunday morning the meeting house became almost unbearable; sweat rolled down solemn faces and there was much mopping of brows. After a while one of the Elders, a Mr. Bobbett, rose and accompanied by sighs of approval made his way to one of the large windows which was only a little open. We waited for him to fling it wide open to let in some air. But no. He closed it tight and resumed his seat. He was aptly named Winter Bobbett.

From *Wallace Litten:*
Recollections of Sidcot Meeting House in the 1920's.

At Sidcot in the early 1920's, our preparation for Sunday morning meeting started on Saturday when we had to show a pair of clean shoes to the housemaster John Thompson (JT). He was a strict disciplinarian and insisted on high standards. After breakfast on Sunday morning there was an opportunity to change reading books in the school library. Then, if the weather was fine, we would parade around the playground trying to memorise a portion from the Bible before a half-hour scripture lesson.

The whole school, about 170 pupils plus staff, attended meeting at 11.0 am. The boys would collect in the boy's shed in height order, and were inspected for tidiness. The girls, having assembled in the playroom, likewise in height order, would make their way across to the Meeting house to take their places on the benches, in the further left-hand half of the room. The boys would follow and sit on the benches in the right-hand half of the room. All in place before 11.00 am. for the one-hour meeting.

The Elders sat on raised seats at the top end of the room, Mr. and Mrs. John Grubb in the back row, with Bevan and Mabel Lean and Lydia Graham. JT sat in a corner front seat keeping his eagle eye on the boys. Christy Burn and Henry Clark sat on the left-hand side. Edward West sat in a left-hand seat and would sometimes tell of interesting times and events during his life at sea. Sercombe Griffin sat on a right-hand wall seat and spoke

THIS CENTURY

Janet and John Thompson, 1934

about his life in Burma.

The Meeting house was heated by large stove in the middle of the room, opposite the door, with a long chimney pipe up through the roof. It could be quite cold away from the stove.

Evening meeting, 6.30-7.15 pm. was a programmed meeting with hymns, readings, taken by senior boys and girls, and a speaker. There was a lectern in the right hand corner from which the speaker addressed us. The Meeting house was also used for school lectures and lantern shows.

It was in 1926 that the Meeting house was enlarged by building on a lobby the full length of the west side of the hall, adding a stage at the south end and putting tiered seats at the north end. Also a small alcove was made on the east side to accommodate a grand piano. When the new hall came into use, an innovation for the scholars was the order of seating on the tiered seats. No longer were boys and girls segregated, but we sat in form order, boys and girls together.

Bevan Lean was justifiably pleased with the new hall, with improved heating arrangements. The stage was separated from the main hall by a fine folding screen with nicely grained natural pine panels. The size of the stage enabled the production of drama on a much improved scale. Olive and I were in the cast of the first production on that stage of Bernard Shaw's St. Joan, the part of Joan being taken by Kitty Trevelyan who was trained by Sybil Thorndyke, a well known actress of that time.

It seems that every one of that time remembers the coke stove. *Kenneth Southall* remembers one occasion when it became red hot and Christie Burn poured cold water on it, causing a sensation. The old stove was abandoned in 1926 in favour of the water heating system we have now.

After the Meeting house had been enlarged, the old forms were replaced by chairs, which caused problems. They considered even putting down rubber or cork flooring, but that was rejected. David Grubb writes in his triennial report for 1927: 'The Seating Accommodation has been much on the minds of Overseers and others, and although several arrangements have been tried, we feel that finality has not yet been reached. The old Friends were indeed fortunate in keeping free from the problem of chairs, and the old-fashioned forms are still held in affectionate memory by many. At any rate they were solid, and in some cases, screwed down, leaving no room for further argument.'

The following was contributed by *Barbara Pask:*

Sidcot Meeting in the 20's and 30's.

My earliest memory of Sidcot meeting is sitting with my feet on a tall hassock of the type used by elderly Friends when kneeling for prayer, an occasion when every one else used to stand.

In front of us sat Mr. and Mrs. West. He was blind, carried a white stick and placed his trilby hat beneath his chair. Next came Mr. and Mrs. Brady who lived at a house in Southmead called "Staindrop". John and Madeline Grubb were Elders, she gave an annual talk about the beauty of Springtime, a theme that we could all understand. Mabel Tothill was a small lady with a round wrinkled face; she lived in Sandford and served both Indian and China tea to visitors sitting out in her lovely garden.

Fanny May, a very large Friend, always dressed in black and white with a large brimmed hat. She went about in a taxi and took people for drives in the country. Then there was "Family Jewels", the name we gave to Mrs. Somers, a tall thin lady who wore long strings of beads, dangling earrings and a purple hat with a silk scarf to match.

Mr. Hitchings was a small stout Yorkshireman with a neat white beard. He cycled from Churchill to meeting and always started his ministry by saying: "When I was a boy at Ackworth...". Many Old scholars remember Dr. Franks who frequently read from a large Bible; his knowledge of it was extensive. He had rather insecure false teeth which gave him a lisp. Marion Chadwick sat just inside the door under the windows and used to report on Meetings for Sufferings. She wore pastel shades of blue and green, a welcome relief from the drab colours favoured by Friends at that time.

When I first went to Sidcot, we sat in Meeting for a full hour, which gave plenty of time to observe the appearance and dress of local Friends who, as now, usually sat in their favourite seats with the Elders facing the tiers .

Edith and Roland Pask arrived in 1923, and both became energetically involved in the life of the Meeting. Edith, as well as restarting the Children's Class, helped to establish the school Junior Meeting in the 1930's, and served on its committee for many years. Both were overseers, and Roland was assistant clerk to Preparative Meeting, and a regular doorkeeper. He was Bursar of Sidcot School from 1923 until 1956.

The Children's Class: The Overseers arranged for a 'Sunday School for the little children of the Meeting' to be held in 1918. Some of the older girls in the school were willing to do the teaching under the guidance of Betty Foster. They held a party in the Meeting house at the end of November and 'the eagerness of the little ones for their Sunday class shows how successfully the work is being carried out.' There were at least fifteen children under twelve in the meeting at that time.

When Edith Pask took over the children's class in 1924, she also enlisted the help of the senior girls, and they went to her each week to prepare for the Sunday lesson. She was still maintaining the same system in 1950 when she gave a report to the P.M. where she showed some of the children's handwork. P.M. decided to make a grant of £3. There were 24 children in children's class at that time She continued looking after the children until the 1970's.

Grace Freem writes: 'In August 1956, when we had been living in Shipham Lane just a few days, Frances and David Murray-Rust came across the fields to welcome us, but as the Sidcot membership at that time was mostly active elderly or "school" I obviously needed to be grabbed as soon as possible for "Sunday School". It was run on formal lines, and followed the Sunday School Union book which was issued annually. The "teachers" I remember were Wallace Litten, Jim Bradley, Joyce Thompson and Joyce Hinton. Some Sidcot scholars helped and they went to Edith Pask each week to prepare for the Sunday lesson and I too was invited, and probably needed it!'

Since Edith Pask there have been several others in charge of the children's class including Joyce Thompson, Joyce Hinton, Katherine Gay, Gillian Hill, and now Daphne Jeffrey, who have done sterling work largely unnoticed by the rest of the meeting, unless they happen to have children of a certain age. However, the new extension and the fact that we have coffee every Sunday in the area where the children are working, has improved things tremendously. There are now about 30 children attached to the meeting but few of them come every week, adding to the difficulties of the teachers. It makes producing a play difficult, too, and Beatrice Vernon (Houghton) followed by Imogen Drakeford have done wonders with their Nativity Plays. Teenagers met once a month at the home of Henry and Lilian Coysh in Hillyfields. Later, when they were too frail to hold their regular classes, some of their former group went to give them some help, and also to enjoy their company. More recently, Tony Cashmore and Bob Drakeford have taken up the concern for the interests of teenagers of the meeting.

Frank Williams recalls Young Friends at Sidcot in the early 1930's:-

A weekend at Sidcot on 2-3 August 1931 was an important event for Young Friends' groups then coming together in the Quarterly Meeting. Hosted by Roland and Edith Pask, the speakers included Rowntree Gillett of Oxford (Home Service Council), Jack Finch of Purley (Young Friends National Secretary), Charles Haworth from Lancashire (social order issues). Young Friends from Friars, Redland, Frenchay, Bath, Taunton, Midsomer Norton were among those accommodated in the school buildings. Some Sidcot folk also attended the sessions. While most of the subject matter has faded after 57 years, I recall that unemployment (especially in South Wales), was a leading feature against the background of the depression. Another, smaller, Young Friends occasion in the thirties was an all-night walk around the Mendips, terminating at the Gibbins' Mendip View bungalow, and a rather sleepy attendance at Sidcot Meeting.

Joshua Watts:-

The 3rd September 1939 was a Sunday. My brother Richard and I returned to school early because it was thought that bombs might fall on Birmingham. We assembled for meeting at 11.00 a.m. as usual, then at 11.15, we adjourned to the school common room, in those days just off the boys' shed, to listen to Mr. Chamberlain make his historic announcement on the wireless. After which we returned to the school hall and meeting continued in the usual way. Certainly a unique occasion.

Evelyn Phillips remembers some people who were in Sidcot Meeting during the war years:-

There were several formidable ladies in the meeting: Evelyn Roberts, Erica Grubb, Mabel Tothill and Lesley Edwards (who lived at Tanemully where midweek meetings were usually held - the name of the house always seemed to amuse the school). Miss Marriage, who lived at Hawkstone, must have been very old. She sat just inside the door. With her heavily powdered

THIS CENTURY

face, she reminded me of Miss Haversham in "Great Expectations".

At the end of the summer term in 1941 the meeting arranged to invite mothers with children under five, from Bristol for a holiday, Bristol having been badly bombed. Some of the mothers turned up with three or four children under five. A number of the school staff stayed on after term ended to help. I helped in the nursery, which was in one of the common rooms. While the mothers were taken on outings, we looked after the little ones, and I grew very fond of one very smelly little baby. Gertrude Dare who was a member of the meeting, gave the mothers a very dramatic account of the well known story of Red Indians' visit to the Quaker Meeting, with much movement and gesture. I can't imagine what the mothers made of it!

Another surprising thing the meeting did was to appoint Richard Brayshaw and me as Elders when we were only in our twenties.

New staff were entertained by members of the meeting. Fiona McQuilty, who was head of the Languages department came to Sidcot when I did, so we were often invited together. Miss Metford and Miss Osborne were two sweet old ladies who lived on either side of Sidcot Lane and we were duly invited to tea by each in turn. Sunday lunch at Mabel Tothill's house in Sandford was a great treat in war time. Visits to the Grubbs at Wintrath were also most enjoyable; they were a wonderful couple and their conversation was so stimulating. Evelyn Roberts and Connie Cameron lived at Prankherds Mead. They had some boys sleeping there, and one of their rooms was also used by the Junior School which was housed at Newcombe. Their upstairs room was a beautiful music room. Of course, Bevan and Mabel Lean were still very much in evidence at this time. Being invited to tea with them felt rather like going for an interview.

On October 2nd 1938 George Hutchinson brought forward the offer of the School Committee to take in refugee children as free day scholars if Friends could take them in as members of their families. By the 6th November, arrangements had been made to accommodate five children. Minutes of P.M. for the 6th June 1941 record the proposal to take in another boy, Kurt Strauss, whose brother Helmut had already been already at the school. Kurt Strauss eventually served on the School Committee as the Old Scholars' representative in the late seventies.

During the war the number of male members of the meeting rose from 55 in 1936 to 80 in 1942, then the numbers began to tail away. The numbers of women were almost constant throughout the war, and several years previously, at about 85. The Meeting reached a peak of 168 members in 1945.

Bill Brown, who was Bursar of Sidcot School from 1957 to 1982, was also Clerk of the Premises Committee for many years. He recalls the two main alterations to the Meeting House in the past thirty years:-

QUAKERS AT SIDCOT

The Meeting House Gallery (1961)

With a steady increase in the number of Sidcot School pupils, the meeting house became uncomfortably overcrowded, and the Committee of Management resolved to seek permission from the Preparative and Monthly Meetings to enlarge it.

Friends were, understandably, not too enthusiastic about a plan to enlarge a room already too big for the meeting's own purposes, but they finally agreed, subject to provision being made for a curtain to close off the gallery when large numbers were not expected. Accordingly, a cavity was formed in the reveal of the arch and a curtain rail was fixed inside, but no curtain was ever fitted. The inevitable bunching that would have resulted when it was drawn open would have made most of the outer tiers of seats unusable.

Before the alterations, there was a single central aisle through the tiers in the Meeting house leading to steps at the north end down to double doors into the north corridor. The seats on the tiers were plain wooden chairs linked by wood battens into sets of four. The depth of each row of the tiers was decided by Bevan Lean. Bevan was large in humanity and intellect but small in stature and particularly in length of leg. He tried out the proposed spacing between the rows and pronounced that it was unnecessarily generous, so tall people have had to sit partly sideways ever since. When seating was planned for the gallery, it was decided to allow rather more kneeroom. Seating in the 'well' was for the most part on wooden benches with very upright backs, and a few scattered cushions which the children were not encouraged to use.

To build the gallery it was first necessary to remove the upper part of the north wall of the meeting room while supporting the edge of the roof. Substantial piers were then built against the east and west walls to support a deep steel joist forty-six feet in length, swung into place by a massive crane on one memorable morning. The corridor roof was reinforced and two rooms were built out beyond the corridor to accommodate the men's lavatory and a 'green room' for stage costumes and properties. The projection room and staircase were removed and the new exterior north wall constructed, joined to the existing building with a lower roof covered with welsh slates to match the original. A wooden framework to support the gallery seating was then constructed, new steps led down to a replanned boiler-room, and a new projection room was built.

The gallery would become very hot when fully occupied and the four long windows provide inadequate ventilation. Two openings were therefore made in the ceiling to allow warm air to escape into the loft space, with wooden grids in the main part of the room. Catwalk access from the gallery vents into the main roof was provided — a most useful provision as previously this space could only be reached with a very tall ladder to the door

THIS CENTURY

set in a dormer above the east wall.

The central aisle of the tiers in the main hall was replaced by the two present aisles, and the wood panelling repositioned. The brass safety rails were added later when users of the the front seats of the gallery complained of vertigo! The architect to the scheme, Paul Kennerel Pope of Bath, designed the benches and seat cushions for the tiers and the gallery in differing lengths to suit their positions. They were expensive, so Friends, parents and Old Scholars were invited to donate them, perhaps as a memorial to a relative. The kneelers were designed and made by David Grubb in the 1960's. Each one is different.

Friends were persuaded to accept the removal of the folding stage screens to allow the depth of the stage to be increased and rather more wing space provided: two of the leaves were then fixed horizontally over the proscenium frame. The old black velvet curtains were replaced and the present ones were the gift of Margaret Nott, who as Margaret Richardson had been Head Girl in 1933/4.'

The North Wing (1984)

The north wing of the meeting house was built originally to house a caretaker and to provide stabling for the horses of visiting Friends: a mounting block at the north west corner was not demolished until the 1930s. The caretaker's accommodation comprised a parlour with a circular staircase to bedrooms above, a kitchen and separate scullery and coal store, with use of the adjacent women's lavatories which were at the east end of the north corridor.

Some years later the stables were converted to form a committee room, with an open shed at the north end which was subsequently walled in to make a lockable storeroom. The caretaker's kitchen became the library in which children's classes were held on Sundays, and her scullery became a kitchen for the meeting house. The internal walls of the parlour were demolished and a door into the adjacent corridor closed off.

No further alterations were made until 1984, when a major scheme was prompted by the necessity to carry out major roof repairs. For some years Friends had wanted to enlarge the committee room so that it could be used for Meetings for Worship when the school was not in session, and to improve the accommodation for the children. The removal of the whole roof gave this opportunity. Premises Committee was asked to prepare a scheme and one of its members (Bill Brown) made a plan and specification. The Monthly Meeting Treasurer launched a local and limited appeal, having obtained the generous promise of a matching gift from an anonymous Quaker trust. A total of £27.500 was obtained in a short time (including the gift from the trust) and this covered almost all the costs.

The land immediately to the east of the north wing formed part of the garden of Somerset Cottage. It was desirable that this should be acquired to give access to the building for ease of maintenance. An exchange was negotiated with the owner of Somerset Cottage, whereby he acquired a narrow piece of the burial ground and a cash adjustment. The land acquired made it possible to fit sliding patio doors from the small meeting room on to a paved area and it gave us the very pleasant view over the fields beyond.

The conversion involved the removal of the wall that separated the north storeroom from the committee room, the demolition of the internal kitchen walls to form an enlarged room for the children's class, the conversion of the women's lavatories into a kitchen with a hatchway into the children's room, and the installation of the women's lavatories in the room off the north corridor, previously used as a 'green room' by the school. The door from the committee room to the children's room was widened, new shelving for the library was put up, and new gas rediators were installed. Fitted carpet was laid throughout and new chairs completed the scheme.

Reminiscences from the 1960s based on notes by Grace Freem and Ruth Fawell:-

Coming from Golders Green Meeting which was very lively and active, Ruth Fawell found our Meeting very static and old fashioned, but one outstanding and dynamic Friend was Helen Neatby (former Headmistress at Sidcot who went to Ackworth and then became Head of of a school in Kenya before returning to Sidcot Meeting); another who gave really live ministry was Richard Cottam. Kitty Franks was another lively minded older Friend. Her husband, Dr. Franks, gave a fully thought out theological address every Sunday, just after the children had left, (which is not the idea in the Society of Friends). He had also led the one study group and Ruth, as an Elder, decided to wean the Meeting from this, and get every Friend willing to lead to take their turn. She found him very kind and understanding about it, and there followed an excellent study group of the prophets, each person choosing one to study.

Richard Brayshaw and Mary Hooper were heads of the School at the time, and they surveyed the whole school when it was in Meeting with eagle eyes, and ruled with a kindly rod of iron.

Ruth continues: 'I remember a great occasion at Evening Meeting when 6th formers took over an "Honest to God" dramatic event. All the interested seniors had been walking about with copies of the book, which excited and stimulated them.' However, as far as Grace was concerned the event that gripped the Preparative Meeting was happening just as Ruth Fawell was leaving for New Zealand (Aotearoa), namely the building of Sewell House.

THIS CENTURY

Sewell House

Late in 1964 Marguerite Sewell had the idea of a home for the elderly in Winscombe. She talked it over with her husband Arnold Sewell and he, in turn, discussed it with Henry Robson whom he happened to meet in the street. Other Friends became interested including Hilda Robson and Arthur Tomlinson, and it was decided to put the concern before Preparative Meeting.

The Preparative Meeting passed the following Minute on 3rd January 1965: 'Arthur Tomlinson has introduced a concern of several members of the meeting that a house should be acquired which could be used as a "Home for the Elderly" of Sidcot Meeting. We welcome this suggestion and appoint the following Committee go into the question: Arthur Tomlinson (who will convene the first meeting), William Brown, Arnold Sewell, Stanley Roberts, Irwin Woodhead, Helen Wills and Annie Cousins. We also suggest that Richard Cottam should be consulted soon after his return to this country later in the month. The Committee has power to seek advice, and suggestions from friends of the Meeting would be welcome.' Richard Cottam was in Africa when this Minute was passed, but he was eager to join the Committee, and became Clerk after Arthur Tomlinson.

A Special Preparative Meeting was held on 19th September 1965, when Richard Cottam gave a report of the Exploratory Committee, as it was then called. He suggested that the type of accommodation envisaged would be mainly in single rooms (with a limited number of double rooms for married couples) each with bed recess, a kitchenette and a wash basin; bathrooms would be shared. It should have a communal dining room for provision of a mid-day meal, one or more communal lounges, warden's accommodation and guest rooms. It should be able to cater for about 25 Friends. It was estimated that the whole project would cost about £45,000, to be met by donations and subscriptions, interest-free loans, the issue of loan stock and loans from Government or Building Societies.

There was also the question of Management with all its responsibilities. The Exploratory Committee became the Interim Committee with Richard Cottam as Clerk; Grace Freem (Clerk to the P.M.), Juliet E. Baker, and Wilson Baker were co-opted. It was decided that a 'Sidcot Friends Housing Society' should be set up, and that discussions should be held with the developer of the Hillyfields Estate which was being developed at that time.

The Committee of Management of the Sidcot Friends Housing Society met for the first time on 12th January 1966; Arnold E. Sewell was Chairman, Arthur Tomlinson was Honorary Treasurer, and Richard Cottam was Honorary Secretary, until the first Annual General Meeting should be held in 1967. After this good start, things began to go wrong, and the conveyance of the site was not signed and sealed until 30th November 1968, and it was the end of July 1969 before building began. The building work was held up too, and when the first tenant took possession of her flatlet in May 1970, she was still surrounded by workmen. Nevertheless, eleven tenants were able to enter the home in May and eight in June, although in fact the work was not satisfactorily completed until April 1971. The house was called "Sewell House", in memory of its first chairman, Arnold E. Sewell, who had died in March 1969.

The extension was built in 1977, enabling six extra tenants to take up residence, and providing more accommodation for the Assistant Warden. In contrast with the building of the main part of the house, it was soon completed and the new flatlets were all occupied by the next January.

A full account of the history of Sewell House can be found in Wilson Baker's book 'Sewell House: Sidcot Friends Housing Society Limited 1965-80'.

Joan Hewitt, who was Assitant Warden for five years until 1979, writes that she was told that, during the electricity power cuts in the early seventies, Edith Pask had carried down to Sewell House a pan of hot soup cooked on her gas stove (she was well in her eighties by then). Stanley Roberts and his wife Evelyn had filled hot water bottles for the tenants during the previous cuts, and he turned up one evening with a basket to collect them. Stanley and Evelyn Roberts were good neighbours in more ways than one, because they allowed residents of Sewell House to walk through their garden which was next door. Before he moved in 1979, he made sure that there was a permanent pathway into Southmead. When John and Edith Robson moved into "Marburg" in 1973, situated at the closed end of Southmead, they also invited Sewell House residents to pass through their garden, so there was an almost direct route through to Apple Tree Drive.

Many residents regularly attend Meeting for Worship and join in Meeting events. The Sewell House Management Committee have also welcomed frequent gatherings there, including the General Interest group held monthly on Friday evenings. Another monthly occasion is the coffee morning which is popular with some of the villagers as well as members of the Meeting, and at which residents have a white elephant stall, where they are also able to sell craft items which they have made, for a variety of good causes. Friends and others in the House, and some members from outside, support the Thursday afternoon meeting for worship there. Some residents also take advantage of another small "branch" of the Meeting, held monthly on Sundays in the home of nearby Friends.

Ruth Fawell eventually returned from New Zealand to live in Sewell House, where she is a very active and valuable member of the community, and the Meeting. A collection of articles written by her over the years, entitled 'Courage to Grow' was published by Quaker Home Service in 1987, around the time of her ninetieth birthday. Another Sidcot Friend whose writings have appeared regularly in 'The Friend' is George Boobyer, whose Biblical knowledge (he was Professor of Theology in Newcastle University) has been a valued feature of his ministry as well as the study groups he led over the years.

The School and the Meeting
by Tom Leimdorfer (Headmaster 1977-86)

When Sidcot was established as a Quaker boarding school in 1808, it became inevitable that the presence of the school would play a major part in the life of the Meeting, determining the type of Meeting House which would be built and unbalancing the composition of worshippers on the Sunday mornings in term time. The possible problems were appreciated from the start, as we read in the 1808 school rules that

> As they (the pupils) will have the advantage of attending at Friends Meeting House when Meetings for Worship are usually held, and considering that those Meetings are for the solemn purpose of worshipping the Almighty, they are enjoined to observe a sober becoming behaviour in going to and returning from them; and more especially when in them, to endeavour after a reverent sense of the awfulness of thus presenting ourselves before our great Creator... .

When we arrived on the scene in 1977, it was clear to me that most pupils were only too aware of the awfulness of having to present themselves before the great Creator on Sunday mornings, but the sense of reverence seemed to be lacking. There was plenty of evidence of 'restless and unbecoming gestures' which the same 1808 rules go on to warn against. And little wonder. The audience of uniformed ranks of up to two hundred and fifty young people looked down on thirty to fifty middle aged and elderly Friends who, try as they may, rarely managed to speak to their condition.

Friends were generally tolerant and those ministering often acknowledged that they themselves felt just as bored and restless at Sidcot, Ackworth, Bootham ... in their youth, but came to appreciate the value of silence in later life. This rarely had the desired effect, and there is wisdom in the advice given in 1934 to 'those who take a vocal part in our meetings' to the effect that

> The Meeting will usually be helped if speakers do not address themselves directly to the boys and girls, but to the whole Meeting as one united group .

The problem, however, is to make the Meeting one united group when most of the young people present would choose to be elsewhere, if given the exercise of free will, and when the oldest of them are normally two decades younger than the youngest member of meeting who is there by choice. Old Scholars abound with tales of placing bets on which member of the meeting would minister, playing games of 'cricket' by awarding runs according to the number of minutes for which the ministry lasted etc.. In 1911, Madeline Grubb complained of the girls' behaviour in Meeting, and it was decided that a mistress should sit at the side. It was not the last complaint, and staff, and particularly Heads would feel that they are present not as worshipping Friends, but as duty policemen distributing disapproving glares during meeting and punishment after it ends.

The obvious remedy of recognising that there can be no such thing as compulsory worship and hence making attendance optional has been proposed many times. George Hutchinson in 1944 proposed that attendance at Meeting should be voluntary and separate arrangements should be made in school for those not wishing to attend. The problem with all such arrangements is that it places extra burden on members on staff on Sunday mornings instead of providing a quiet oasis in a busy week. In fact, several members of staff have given sterling service over the years in organising or leading Junior Meeting or Middle School Meeting. In recent years, Tony Cashmore, David Lindley, Grace Hopes, Desmond Harris, Jenny Sisman, Rachel Stainer have been amongst those who felt a special concern for such meetings.

The present arrangement emerged after discussion involving Elders, school staff and the School Committee in March 1980. The aim was to reduce the number of pupils attending on any one Sunday, to try to integrate them in the body of the meeting amongst Friends and to make them feel part of the Meeting. It was felt that some element of compulsory attendance was justifiable on the grounds that pupils attending a Quaker school should have some experience of Quaker Meeting. Every effort should be made, however, that their presence does not prevent it from being a Meeting for Worship. So juniors, middle school and seniors all attend on a different Sunday in the month, leaving one Sunday each month clear even in term time. A few pupils come voluntarily on that Sunday. The requirement to wear school uniform was dropped in 1982. There was an increase in the number of small group meetings at the homes of members of staff, more junior and middle school meetings and a monthly fifth form meeting was organised by Jean Plant. Grumbles by Friends about the school and by the pupils about the meeting were greatly reduced.

There have been several successful attempts at increasing informal contacts between the school and members of the meeting such as fifth and sixth form socials and the occasional discussion evenings. The first sixth form social was at The Down, the home of John and Madeline Grubb in 1919. In more recent times they were held at Eleanor Gage's studio and then at Hampden, the home of Howard and Jennifer Knight. A few pupils have been regular visitors at Sewell House and some lasting friendships have been formed. Throughout this century, Friends have appreciated being invited to school plays, concerts and Sunday Evening Meetings, though there have been times when members of the meeting found the school play disturbingly modern or 'un-Quakerly'. On other occasions, the performance inspired thoughtful ministry on the following morning.

It cannot be doubted that, for all the ups and downs of the relationship between the school and the meeting, both have benefited greatly. Several members of staff, parents and quite a few pupils have joined Friends. A few students, and not only sixth formers, have been moved to minister very acceptably. Many have found the silence helpful, even healing. Most take away something of lasting value.

The Autumn Sale
In 1931 the Friends Service Council asked that the week beginning November 22nd should set apart as an 'F.S.C.' week. It was decided that a special collection should be taken on November 22nd, and a bring and buy sale should be held. The collection realised £5.3.1, and the sale £10.7.4.

The sale stopped during the war, and only became a regular occasion again around 1950. When the Friends Service Council combined with Friends Peace and International Committee in 1979 to become Quaker Peace & Service, it became the 'QPS Sale'. More recently, its scope was extended to raise funds for all aspects of Quaker work, so it is now the 'Sale in Aid of Quaker Work'. It has become the main fund raising occasion of the year, and the November 1989 sale raised £1440. It is a grand team effort by many helpers which was co-ordinated for several years by Joyce Hinton before Ethel Waller took over the task. The November Sale is supplemented in Spring by the Jumble Sale and for several years there was an annual coffee morning a sale of work at the home Howard and Jennifer Knight at the end of the summer term.

QPS Sale 1985

Other Fund Raising Activities

Other fund raising events ranged from a concert by the school arranged by Edward Davis and Rosemary Blomfield in aid of F.S.C. in 1945, to a stawberry tea in Sandra MacQueen's beautiful garden in 1989. In recent years some of Friends' more traditional causes have been taken up more widely by larger bodies. It might be said that, as in the Society generally, Sidcot Friends have adopted less popular causes, such as help for victims of crime and rehabilitation of offenders, or small projects in Northern Ireland. On fifth Sundays, however, we still have a collection for a disaster fund.

There is still coffee served at the market every Thursday without fail, which raises a regular income. Jean Ironside holds regular meetings in her house for making reconstituted and pressed flower cards. These are also made at Sewell House.

Walks and Picnics
by David Lindley

'As far as our records show, the walks started on 24 September 1978, as an idea put forward by Jean Ironside and the Overseers while Joan Williams was clerk. Richard and Joyce Hinton were our first hosts at Penhalt.

The Winscombe area being so well endowed with footpaths, the majority of walks have been local, and the leader has usually, but not always, been one of the hosts. We are grateful to our many hosts who have opened up their houses

Walking past Pankherds Mead, 1985

Jennifer Knight and Charlotte Allen at Hampden, 1983

and gardens for our picnics. Local houses we visited have included those of Wilson and Juliet Baker, Desmond and Cristine Boobyer, Aubrey and Gillian Hill, Don and Jean Ironside, Edward and Daphne Jeffree (both at Honey Hall and Winscombe), Howard and Jennifer Knight (where the most hardy amongst us could enjoy a swim), and Tom and Valerie Leimdorfer, when they lived at Sidcot. In the earlier days, Eleanor Gage's Studio was a welcome destination.

We have had some very enjoyable walks further afield. We have been more than once to Zoe Gertner at her Bagley Studio. We have visited Ethel Waller at Westbury-sub-Mendip, Ena Mogridge and Robert at Burrington, and Desmond and Barbara Simonds at Brinsea. The furthest afield was to Ken and Jean Plant's home in the Cotswolds, and we also visited them when they lived at Newcombe.

We were able to explore the Goblin Combe area as a result of Marjorie Mallik's invitation to finish and picnic at Claverham Meeting House. There were memorable days at the home of Esmie and Laurie Ricks after exploring the Blagdon Reservoir area, and finishing with a fund-raising picnic.'

I remember the time when Laurie showed us the site of the old Butcombe Burial Ground, now just the corner of a grass field. I had almost a feeling of awe as I stood there with other members of the meeting. I thought of all those old Friends who were buried there and it seemed like a bridge across the centuries.

Let us return to David Lindley's memories: most of the walks have been during the summer but,
'Tony Cashmore has, on several occassions, led a New Year's Day walk, one year, we walked over snow-covered Wavering Down and Shute Shelve tunnel festooned with massive icicles.

QUAKERS AT SIDCOT

We have to thank Juliet Baker and Grace Freem for organising the walks. They have been instrumental, amongst others, in providing us with many social, health improving, happy hours. Our groups have included Sewell House, wall-climbing octogenarians, to families with babes in back packs. Our fellowship and knowledge of each other have increased immeasurably.'

The Sidcot Panel of the Quaker Tapestry
by Grace Taplin

The conception of the Quaker Tapestry scheme came to a Friend (Anne Wynn-Wilson) when she was working with a small group of children in Taunton in 1981. Her idea was that it could be a ten-year project for communication and education through the medium of embroidery.

She presented the idea to the Children and Young People's Committee of Quaker Home Service in 1982. The first panel depicting George Fox's convincement was exhibited at Yearly Meeting at Warwick in 1982, and it was immediately obvious that Friends were enthusiastic.

Friends were then asked to submit suggestions for subjects to be included in the tapestry scheme and over 400 were received. The selection of 60 panels, each

Sidcot panel of the Quaker Tapestry

THIS CENTURY

measuring 21"x24", was made by members of a newly-formed committee, after much prayerful thought about this important task. More subjects have since been added, and the number now amounts to 76.

The Bayeux Tapestry was the inspiration behind the Quaker Tapestry. The style was not copied, but stitches and techniques were selected to allow over a thousand embroiderers of different ages and abilities, working in widely scattered groups, to co-operate. A new corded stitch was invented for the lettering, and this new stitch has been accepted by The Royal School of Needlework and is officially known as "Quaker Stitch".

Our Sidcot panel depicts the Friends Ambulance Unit:- "A record of goodwill and positive service by conscientious objectors in twenty-five countries as a result of war". Here in Winscombe we were very fortunate when doing our research as we have a Friend (Arthur Marsden) who joined the F.A.U. in 1915 at the age of 17. Another Friend (Bill Brown) served in the F.A.U. in the Second World War. More could be said about the workshops, the humorous little incidents, and most important, the getting to know each other more by spending time together working quietly. Our Sidcot tapestry panel was completed on Saturday, 21st January 1989.

Sidcot Meeting now ... and then

I have hardly touched on all the different study groups that take place during the winter months. The 'Gifts and Discoveries' Study Pack has meant a lot of work and new insights for some members of the Meeting. The fortnightly Prayer Support and Healing Group at Sewell House is a small group which I for one feel is very supportive. Then we have the annual 'bring and share' New Year party, the summer outings to various places of interest organised each year by Olive and Wallace Litten, and the Craft mornings at Jean Ironside's house. The meeting provides the backbone of the East/West Friendship Group, which had as its predecessor the Sidcot Peace Action Group and its offshoot the Sidcot Esperanto group which has now joined up with the Woodspring Esperanto Group. These are just some of the things one can do in one's spare time!

Sidcot is a most active meeting by any standard. But what would Timothy Willis, John Dory,, William Lawrence, John Lovell, William Reeve and the rest of our founders in 1690 make of it all? They certainly did not expect time to stand still. After all, the original meeting house was handed to the trustees for 1000 years for the use of the people 'now called Quakers by what name or names, title or titles of Distinction soever they may hereafter be called'. So perhaps they would be surprised that after 300 years we are still called Quakers!

They would, no doubt be delighted by the numerical strength of the meeting. Some of our social activities might not meet their approval, at least they would marvel at some of our frivolities. They would envy our freedom from persecution, perhaps they would find us all too cosy and comfortable in our ways and possibly too well adapted to the ways of the world. However, I feel sure that they would find our concerns for justice and peace and for preserving the integrity of God's creation close to their hearts. No doubt, they would be saddened to find that three hundred years after the Battle of the Boyne (fought just a couple of months after Sidcot Meeting was established) we should still need to pray for peace in Ireland. The horrors of the wars in this century would seem incomprehensible to them, but they would no doubt rejoice with us at the present time of easing of tensions in Europe.

There were times in our history when our forbears seemed to have prophetic insight. As early as 1737, the Yearly Meeting epistle advised Friends: 'in the Education of their children, take care, as suitable opportunity and occasions may offer, to let them be instructed in some modern Tongue, as French, high & low Dutch, Danish etc. that so when they are grown up, they themselves, if Traders to foreign Countrys may reap the benefit thereof; and as it shall please the Lord to dispose & incline them, may be of benefit to the Church'.

Now, some 250 years later, the National Curriculum is making the learning of a foreign language compulsory, in preparation of the common European market of 1992. I feel sure that the Friends who drafted that would approve not only of the activities of our Esperanto group, but the numerous international links which the meeting has made by travels of its members to all corners of the world and by warmly welcoming visitors from all continents.

Visitors, whether they are parents of pupils at the school, old scholars, Friends from other meetings, or friends of members of our own meeting, are very much a feature of Sidcot life. So it is quite hard to spot the newcomer who may have come to Meeting for the first time as an enquirer, perhaps after a long spiritual journey and much heartsearching. One such enquirer, now a member of our meeting recalls that, when she and her husband came for the first time after moving into the area: 'Sidcot Friends made us most welcome, made no demands and accepted us "as we were" without any reservations. This seemed a good time to make a new start - we felt at home at Sidcot'. For others, feeling at home takes a little longer and meetings and study groups for enquirers are organised from time to time for discussions.

Overseas visitors help to remind us that the world has shrunk dramatically as we moved from travel by horseback and hazardous sea crossings to motor cars, supersonic jets and satellite communication. We have both gained and lost much in the process. We may well marvel at how early Friends managed to fit in so many long meetings and travel so far at so slow a pace. How did they have so much time? Why are we always short of time?

There are many imponderables as we try to span three centuries, but there is one unbreakable common thread. The diverse outward activities of Friends then, as now, were centred on the same humble search for Truth, the same silent listening for 'the still small voice' in our hearts, the same meeting in a healing silence and then going forth 'to walk cheerfully over the earth, meeting that of God in everyone'. May it continue for the next three hundred years and beyond!

Left to Right Front Row
*Will and Gwen Cushnie, Vi Brown, Franceys Longman, Jean Ironside,
Esmie Ricks, Rebecca Schwartz, Barbara Robson, Edith and John Robson*

Left to Right Second Row
*Aubrey Hill, Bill Brown, Donald Ironside, Hilda Short,
David Curtis, Laurie Ricks, Margaret Hawkes.*

THIS CENTURY

Left to Right on Ground, First Row:
Jennifer Batten, Lucy Stainer, Emma Sinnet, Amelia Bamford, David Burge, Sophie Stainer, George Greenfield.

Left to Right, Second Row:
Bryony Bamford, Alice Stainer, David Drakeford, Matthew Haynes, Timothy Sinnet, Philippa Drakeford, Clare Nicol, Vicky Nicol, Sarah Burge, Jennifer Litten.

Seated on the Wall:
Susan Collins, Susan Bamford, Imogen Drakeford, Margaret Johnson.

Seated on Chairs:
Barbara Pask, Margaret King, Ruth Fawell, Valerie Leimdorfer, Joan Williams, Olive and Wallace Litten, Juliet and Wilson Baker, Christopher Greenfield.

Standing behind Wall:
Marlies Dufour, Aubrey and Grace Hopes, Margaret Batten, Irene Threasher, Ross Wallis.

Standing behind First Row:
Edward and Daphne Jeffree, Helen Perry-Smith, Kay Baker, Katherine Gay, Tom Leimdorfer, Beryl Francis, Frank Williams, Eleanor Gage, Diane Litten, Jean Salisbury, Jane Burge, Rachel Stainer.

Standing behind Second Row:
Peter and Grace Taplin, Philip Batten, Kirsty MacQueen, Kenneth Baker, Ethel Waller, Sandra MacQueen, Basil Francis, David Nicol, Linda Batten, Joyce Lindley, Winifred Booker, Janet Arnold, Gillian Greenfield, Joyce Hinton, Peter Bowyer.

Back Row:
Chris. and Robert Myers, Rosalind Cashmore, Adam MacQueen, Phillip Packer, David Lindley, Christopher Batten, Valerie Major, James MacQueen, Malcolm Litten, Rosalind Sinnet, Duncan Stainer, Richard Hinton.

APPENDIX I

SOME OF THE ACTS OF PARLIAMENT UNDER WHICH QUAKERS SUFFERED

In 1512, in the 27th year of the reign of King Henry VIII, a law was made for payment of Tithes. The Judge of an Ecclesiastical Court could make a complaint to two Justices of the Peace in a suit for Tithes, and the Justices could commit the defendant to prison until he could give sufficient evidence that he would obey the court's ruling.

At the beginning of Queen Elizabeth's reign a law was made for the administering of the Oath of Supremacy of the Monarch.

In the first year of Queen Elizabeth's reign there was an Act for the Uniformity of Common Prayer and Church Service which contained this clause, 'Every person shall resort to their Parish Church ..... every Sunday and Holiday, upon pain to be punished by Censures of the Church, and also to forfeit twelve pence by the Churchwardens there, for the Use of the Poor'.

About 22 years later another law was made relating to the above Act. A fine of £20 per month was levied for non-attendance at Church, and if they did not go to Church for 12 months they could be bound over for sureties of £200 and not released until they started to attend Church according to above Act.

In the 29th of Queen Elizabeth's reign (1587) a law was made allowing seizure of 'all the goods and two third Parts of the Lands and Leases of every offender not repairing to Church as aforesaid'.

In the 35th year of Elizabeth's reign an Act was passed that anyone over 16 should be imprisoned if they absented themselves from Church for more than a month, impugned the Queen's Authority in Ecclesiastical Causes, frequented Conventicles (meetings or assemblies) or persuaded others to do so, under pretence or exercise of Religion. If within three months after such a conviction they refused to conform they were required to swear in open court to leave the country for ever.

In the third year of James I, (after the discovery of the Gunpowder Plot in 1605), an Act was made enjoining the taking of the Oath of Allegiance.

Although these laws were all made against the Catholics, they could be used equally well against Quakers, but there were also Acts made specifically against Quakers. In 1661 an 'An Act for Preventing Mischiefs and Dangers that may arise by certain Persons called Quakers and others refusing to take Lawful Oaths'. By this Act not only was it unlawful to refuse to take an Oath before a lawful Magistrate, or to try to persuade others that it was against the Word of God, but was unlawful for five or more to assemble together in any place 'under pretence of Religious Worship'. The penalty for the first offence was not more than £5, for the second £10, and for non-payment of fines, prison, and hard-labour. For the third offence the punishment was Transportation. In 1664 there was a similar Act making it unlawful to hold such a meeting on one's property.

In 1665 the 'Five Mile Act' prevented non-conformist ministers from preaching or even living within five miles of any corporate or Parliamentary borough, unless they took an oath that they would never attempt any alteration in Government, Church or State.

In 1670 another Act to prevent conventicles caused much suffering for Friends. No jury was required and a single Justice could convict. Heavy fines were levied on those who preached in such assemblies or allowed their homes to be used for such a purpose. A third of the fine went to the Informer, so Friends were at the mercy of anyone who was willing for malice or money to inform against them. The fines could be recovered by distraining goods, so many Quakers were reduced to poverty, as all goods became prey to informers.

The year 1672 showed a lessening of persecution as King Charles II issued a declaration for suspending the Penal Laws in relation to Ecclesiastic matters. After this 491 Quakers were released from prison and pardoned, but the interlude did not last long, and the following year Parliament insisted that the King withdraw the Declaration.

Quakers lost no time in petitioning James II, when he came to the throne in 1685. He gave instruction that no more writs were to be issued against Quakers for non-attendance at public worship, and Informers were gradually discontinued. At last, in 1687, the King made a 'Declaration for Liberty of Conscience', which eased the suffering considerably, but it was not supported by an Act of Parliament, so the liberty granted was very uncertain.

In 1689, in the reign of King William III and Queen Mary came the 'Act for exempting their Majesties Protestant subjects, dissenting from the Church of England, from the Penalties of Certain Laws'-The Act of Toleration.

The Corporation Act (1661) and the Test Act (1673) which insisted that all public officials and municipal officers should be members of the Church of England were not repealed until 1828. The five mile Act was repealed in 1811. In 1868 the abolition of Church Rates relieved non-conformists of the necessity of paying for the upkeep of Parish Churches.

APPENDIX II

KINGS AND QUEENS OF ENGLAND FROM ELIZABETH I

Elizabeth I	1558-1603	George I	1714-27
James I	1603-25	George II	1727-60
Charles I	1625-49	George III	1760-1820
Oliver Cromwell's Protectorate 1649-60		George IV	1820-30
Charles II	1660-85	William IV	1830-37
James II	1685-88	Victoria	1837-1901
William III	1688-1702	Edward VII	1901-10
& Mary II	1688-94	George V	1910-36
Anne	1702-14	Edward VIII	1936
		George VI	1936-52
		Elizabeth II	1952-

APPENDIX II
THE ELEVEN PARTICULARS 1698 (much summarised)

1. No unnecessary things at marriages or burials, in meat, drink nor apparel.
2. Deal tenderly and in time with those tending to seek husbands or wives not professing truth.
3. Deal with those neglecting meetings, week day, monthly and quarterly as well as first day, or sleeping in meeting. Parents and Masters to advise their children and servants to diligence. Friends to come orderly together at the time appointed.
4. No payment of tithes, either direct or underhand.
5. Use plain language. Parents should set a good example to children.
6. No observation of the vain customs or foolish fashions of the people of the world, nor speaking evil of each other behind their backs.
7. Deal with all tatlers and tale bearers who sow discord among us, until it becomes known to the people of the world.
8. No unnecessary frequenting of alehouses
9. Deal with those who join in feasts, games, sights and shows which stir the light and vain mind to laughter, madness and folly.
10. Care that all in trade or employment do not exceed their capacity, deal honestly and pay their debts, also they should not maintain extravagent expenses in keeping company above their rank.
11. Care for the truly poor, who should be diligent in honest employment, otherwise they should not expect help from Friends.

One more particular was added later:

12. That all Friends avoid keeping servants who are not Friends, because of their wordly influence on children. Also that Friends' children should not go into service with people of the world

APPENDIX III

MINUTES OF THE MONTHLY MEETING AT WOODBOROUGH THE 1ST OF THE 6TH MONTH 1701

(at William Reeve's)

Friends present: Wm. Reev, Wm. Lovell (Havyatt), Charles Rogers (Frome), Richard Hipsly (Stock), Samuel Romney (Walton-in-Gordano), James Plumly (Priddy), John Hipsley (Chew Magna), Wm. Jenkins (Sidcot), John Cowling (Brislington?, Stanton Drew or Walcot), Thomas Davis (Congresbury), James Hobbs (Portishead), Robert Sharp (Nailsea or Portishead), Jasper Batt (Street), Abraham Thomas (Winthill, Banwell), Tho. Reeve (Woodborough), Richard Thomas (Flax Bourton or Backwell), Wm. Goodridge (Winthill), Robert Blanch (Brislington or Whitchurch), John Lovell (Wrington), Samuel Thomas (Barrow Gurney).

To this meeting was brought a letter from John Barnes stuffed with abundance of confused arguments: & was read but friends thinking it not worth answering for severall reasons & particularly because he have owned himself to be a member of Bristoll and have not yeat brought us any certificates thereof & friends have appointed John Cowling & Robert Blanch to speak with the sayd John Barnes and to give him the sence of the meeting on this matter.

To this meeting was brought the Epistle from the last yearly meeting at London and read and endorsed to be read in the several meetings belonging to our Monthly Meeting.

Whereas Daniell Hollister did at our monthly meeting at Bath the 30th of the 3rd Month propose his Intention of Marriag with Mary Reeve Daughter of John Reeve: which in order to have a Certificate. Robert Blanch Gives an account of his clearness from all other persons on account of Marriage as also of his walking pretty orderly amongst Friends, a Certificate is ordered to be given him to satisfie friends in Bristoll where the sayd marriage is intended to be consummated, also Robert Blanch testifies that the sayd Mary Gives her Consent to the above sayd proposall.

Friends doe agree that a publick testimony be given for against Judith Sayer and it is left to Wm. Reeve and Wm. Jenkins to draw up the sayd testimony which is ordered, a Coppy of it is to be read to the sayd Judith and it is left to John Cowling and John Hipsly to take care abut it to see to get it don.

Charles Rogers of Froome, being disposed to remove from there into Bristol, have desired a Certificate from our own Meeting and Friends have left the matter to John Davis and John Clare to make enquiry as touching the sayd Charles, his Clearness in his removall and to give Friends an account at our next meeting.

APPENDIX IV

Dispersed to the us of the poore and other servise -	£	s	d
Repayd to John Cowling monys that he disbursed to the reliff of the widdow Little in the time of her lameness		6	0
pd. John Cowling that he layd out for som accs of parliment		1	6
sent Joane Chapman by Rob. Blanch for 2 months		10	0
sent by Robert Blanch to Roger Walker		3	0
sent by Robert Sharp to Rebecah Streting		5	0
sent by Wm. Lovell for Sarah Beess for 3 months		7	6
sent by Rich. Thomas for Sarah Michell		5	0
Repayd to Abraham Thomas that he gave to Mary Jenings		2	6
payd to Wm Jenkins pursuant to the order of the Quarterly Meeting	2	14	0
Totall	4	14	6

The next Monthly Meeting is Appointed to be at Winthill at the hous of Abraham Thomas at the usuall time.

John Barnes had caused trouble before (1695). When his ministry became a burden to Friends of Keynsham Meeting he was persuaded to be silent. This time he was found 'pretty mild' and he was left with his letter and ordered to burn it.

The intentions of marriage were usually were near the beginning of the Meeting. Mary Reeve was from Bristol; Daniel Hollister was from Whitchurch.

Judith Sayer (of Worle?) had gone to a priest to be married and 'brought a scandall on the profession of truth'.

Nothing much is known of the women who received payments.

APPENDIX IV

Quarterly Meeting Queries recommended by Yearly Meeting in 1755:-

1. Are Meetings for Worship & Discipline Duly attended ... and do Friends avoid all unbecoming behaviour therein;
2. Are love and Unity preserved amongst you & 'do you discourage all talebearing & Detraction;
3. Is it your care by example & precept to train up your Children in a Godly

Conversation & in frequent reading the holy scriptures, and also in plainness of speech, behaviour and apparell;
4. Do you bear a faithful & Chritian Testimony against the receiving or paying Tythes, Priests Demands, or those called Church rates;
5. Are Friends careful to avoid all vaine sports, places of diversion, gaming and all unnecessary frequenting of all alehouses, or taverns, excess in drinking and intemperance of every kind;
6. Are Friends just in Dealings & punctual in fulfilling their engagements;
7. Is early care taken to advise & deal with such as appear inclineable to marry contrary to ye rules of our Society, & do no Friends remove from or into your Meetings or Two Weeks Meetings without certificate;
8. Have you two or more faithful friends deputed in each particular Meeting to have oversight thereof, and is care taken when anything appears amiss that the rules of our discipline be put into practice;
9. Do you keep a record in your Meetings and Quarterly Meetings of the prosecutions and sufferings of your respective members, and have you a record for your Meeting Houses and Burial Grounds, and is due care taken to register all Marriages, Births and Burials.

This was a time when the Queries were the main touchstone for administering the discipline of the Society. In earlier days (1682-1700), the three original queries ('What friends ... departed this life since the last Yearly Meeting? What friends...have died in prison...? How the Truth has prospered among them since the last Yearly Meeting, and how friends are in peace and unity?') were asked at each Yearly Meeting and oral replies given by Quarterly Meeting representatives. There were revisions at various times and 'General Advices' were first added in 1791. The current 'Advices and Queries' date from 1964 and a revision process is under way at the time of writing with a provisional document entitled 'Questions and Counsel' in use for a trial period.

APPENDIX V
List of Clerks from 1847

Compiled from P.M. Minutes.
1847-52	John Frank
1852-58	Henry Lees
1858-59	Henry Dymond
1859-60	Francis Wm. Wood
1860-61	Joseph Theobold
1861-68	Josiah Evans
1868-69	Benjamin Gouch
1869-71	John Sharp
1871-75	Robert M. Lidbetter
1875-86	?

Compiled from Book of Mtgs.
1886-1902	Joseph Lane
1903-06	John Grubb
1907-11	Annie Amelia Burn
1912-13	C. F. Spencer Smith
1914-16	Lydia S. Graham
1917-20	Annie Amelia Burn
1921-23	Isabel Grubb
1924	John Grubb
1925-26	Henry R. Clark
1927-28	David B. Grubb
1929-33	Gerald Littleboy
1934-37	Cecil Gibbins
1938-40	Helen I. Wills
1941-42	Henry I. Robson
1943-51	Margaret R. Shanks
1952-56	Frances Murray-Rust
1957-60	H. Wallace Litten
1961-62	J. William Farrell
1963-66	Grace M. Freem
1967-70	Joan M. Cottam
1971-78	Thomas R. King
1979-81	Donald Ironside
1982-85	Daphne Jeffree
1986-89	Joyce Hinton
1989	Richard Hinton
1990-	Margaret Batten

Tom King, one of the longest-serving P.M. Clerks, who inspired the idea of writing this book; picture taken in 1979

QUAKERS AT SIDCOT

North Somerset M.M. (1668-1876)
North Somerset & Wilts. M.M. (1876-
List of Clerks from 1873

-1873	Josiah Evans (Sidcot=S)
1874-1876	Henry Barron Smith
1876-1878	Edward Sturge
1879-1880	Irwin Sharp
1881-1896	Edmund Ashby S
1897	William Robinson
1898-1902	William Kitching S
1903-1918	Edmund Ashby S
1919-1923	C. Lilian Burcham S
1924-1926	Eustace H. Clothier S
1927-1929	Richard Beck
1930-1934	Charles A. Marsh
1935-1939	Cecil Gibbins S
1940-1945	Mary Owen
1946-1950	C. Ivan Gray S
1951-1954	J. F. Henry S. Mussell
1955-1956	Ralph Dixon
1957-1961	Bernard J. Banner S
1962-1965	Charles Gray S
1966-1967	Geoffrey W. Pilliner
1968-1970	John Arnold S
1971-1975	Richard Cottam S
1976-1980	John C. Bailey
1981-1983	George Hather
1984-1986	J. Desmond Simonds S
1986-1988	Herbert Bell
1989-	Angela Courtney

APPENDIX VI

P.M. ACCOUNTS 1988

1987	Current A/C	
1213	Contributions (MM/PM)	2312
61	Interest	222
51	Donations	93
1052	Other Income	105
2377		2732
	Expenses	
400	School for upkeep	—
154	Officers' expenses	135
1670	Donations	140
78	Library and posters	113
3	Repairs & equipment	103
—	Children's Class	107
2384	Other	110
4689		708
(2312)	Under/overspent	2024
2422	Balance at start	242
110	Balance at end	2266
132	Net transfer	(2143)
242	Balance C/F	123
	Deposit A/C	
191	Balance B/F	354
2263	Added	9566
2454		9920
2100	Withdrawn	6710
354	Balance C/F	3210
	Bristol & West Bdg. Soc.	
	Deposit A/C	6000

1987	2nd A/C Central Fund	
41	Balance B/F	36
217	Market Coffee	208
—	Aft. Mtg. Coffee	74
112	Gifts	44
99	Boxes	53
121	Chil'n Concert & Sale	159
318	Jumble Sale	221
100	Coffee Morning	152
1184	Nov. Sale	1377
7	Diaries	86
105	Sewell House cards	90
—	Aft. Mtg. Sales	45
—	Interest	32
32	Other Income	75
2336		2652
—	Diaries	93
2300	To Central Fund	2500
2300		2593
36	Balance C/F	59
	3rd A/C Alterations	
603	Balance B/F	1346
1875	Added	7
2478		1353
1132	Withdrawn	1353
1346	Balance C/F	=
	Account closed	

LIST OF MEMBERS OF SIDCOT MEETING

The following lists represent an attempt to collect the names of all those who have been members of the meeting or have been closely associated with it. Inevitably, it is incomplete. The earliest published list of members for North Somerset and Wiltshire M.M. which I could consult was for 1875. A blue piece of paper with the list of members for 1870 was inserted in the back of the book containing the P.M. minutes for that year. The only earlier list was found in the back of the Monthly Meeting minutes of 1830-46. In order to compile the list, I read through Monthly Meeting minutes from 1667 and noted down the names of all Friends who were associated with Sidcot. For the early years, up to 1699, Stephen Morland's notes proved to be a most useful source.

This means, that Friends whose names never featured as representatives to Monthly Meeting and were not mentioned in some other context (certificate of transfer, marriage, discipline, receipt of money, death etc.) are likely to be missing. From 1875 onwards, published lists were used, but these were not available for every year. Hence Friends who were associated with the meeting for only a short time could be missing even from the 20th century lists.

The lists are in two parts. The first list includes members up to and including 1921. It is an alphabetical list, but Friends with the same surname are listed in approximate chronological order, which may help in tracing families such as the the Hipsleys and the Tanners. This list contains some abbreviated historical notes. The second list was compiled by Aubrey Hill from Quarterly and then General Meeting lists from 1921 onwards, omitting those who were already members in 1921. Friends with the same surname are listed in alphabetical order of first names, but families are kept together.

LIST OF MEMBERS OF SIDCOT MEETING
(AND OTHERS ASSOCIATED WITH THE MEETING)

b. born, m. married, d. died, ch. children, s. son of, d. daughter of, w. widow of, a. attender
§ Member of the Sidcot School Staff, [a] associate member,
non-members are enclosed in brackets []
MM. Monthly Meeting, PM. Preparative Meeting, GM. General Meeting
app. applied, appr. apprentice, appt. appointed, cert. certificate,
Fit - 'Friends judged meet to keep the men's meetings'
Mtg. Meeting, MH. Meeting House, nr. near, rec. received, reg. regular
rep. representative, sev. several, SS. Sidcot School, test. testify

§ ABBATT William
    m. Maria Lucas of Sibford 1852
ABRAM Jane. Poor Friend 1713
ADDAMS Thomas of Clutton
    m. Judith Farmer of Sidcot, 1708
§ ADDEY Alfred William, listed in 1879
§ ADE Frank C. a.,listed 1919.
§ ALEXANDER William Henry, junior master in SS. 1881
ALEXANDER Ellen a. with 4 ch. 1st listed 1896
    On list of reps. for M.M. 1903.
    Lived at Winterhead Hill Farm with husb. Henry A.
    Moved to Koeings Post Office, Shawnigan Lake,
    Vancouver Island, B.C..
ALEXANDER Mabel a. 1st listed 1901
ALEXANDER Norman, Keately P.O., Saskatchewan, Canada. Listed 1913.
    Moved to Koeing's P.O., Shawnigan Lake, Vancouver Island, B.C..
ALEXANDER Florence a. listed 1907.
ALEXANDER Margaret a. listed 1907.
ALEXANDER Katherine M., White Cottage, Shipham, listed 1921.
ALEXANDER Theodore, White Cottage, Shipham, listed 1921.
ALLBRIGHT William jnr.. Shopkeeper
    m. Rachel Tanner d. Wm. snr. and Hannah, at Sidcot 1801.
ALLEN George s. John (of Yatton) d.1722
    m. Lydia Thomas d. Abraham and Grace , at Sidcot 1718
ALLEN Lydia w. George
    m.2 Samuel Horwood of Nailsea
ALLEN John of Yatton, Yeoman
    reg. at MM. Claverham Overseer
    m.1 Joan Rumney 1694
    m.2 Joan Davis of Rowbarrow 1699
AMESBURY Elizabeth of Shiplett (d. Richard of Huntspill)
    m. John Payne of Broad Marson, at Sidcot 26-5-1761
ANDREWS Hannah - a poor young woman 1745 (prob. of Chew)
ARSCOTT Alexander - mentioned in relation to the difference between Wm.Jenkins
    and Webb Davis, 1724
§ ASHBY Edmund, head of SS. 1873-1902

QUAKERS AT SIDCOT

§ ASHBY Eliza, mistress of SS. 1873-1902
    Moved to Clevehead, Cross, nr. Axbridge, 1902
    with Alice, Margaret and Howard.
ASHBY Charles, s. Edmund and Eliza, moved away 1899
ASHBY Frederick Oswald., 2nd s. Edmund and Eliza, d. of consumption 1896.
ASHBY Edith Gertrude. d. Edmund and Eliza b. between 1870 and 1874.
ASHBY Elizabeth of Laurel Cottage, on list of membs. 1875.
ASHBY Rebecca Mary of Arno Cottage, on list of membs. 1875.
    ch. Hannah Elizabeth
ASHBY Howard, Cleevehead, Cross, Nr. Axbridge, (see above) listed 1901.
    [m. Jessie Maud]
ASHBY Francis, Prankherd's Mead, Sidcot. Listed 1906.
    Elizabeth
        ch. Lucy Elizabeth
            Eva Caroline
            Rosamond Lucas
            Ruth Kathleen
            Phyllis Constance
            John Eric.
ASHBY Margaret (w. of Samuel) 5 South Hill, Sandford, listed 1921
ASHLEY Jessie a., listed 1917
ATHEYS John of Winscombe
    m. by Priest 1710. Test. against.
AUSTIN Susan of Banwell
    m. William Croy of Sidcot 1695
AUSTIN Mabel a., listed 1909.
AVERY Albert, a. 1st mentioned 1892

BAKER John of Burrington   d.1689
    m. Mary   d.1686
    reg. at MM.
BAKER William (of Sidcot Mtg.) moves to Frenchay 1713
§ BAKER William, appr. at SS. about 1840
BALKWILL Harriet, Clanville. Listed 1919.
BALLET Gabriel of Blackford in Wedmore, Husbandman.
    m. Mary Tugwell of Winscombe. 1691
    He broke his leg in an accident at Sidcot, 1709
BANE George - lived in Claverham MH. and disturbed mtg. 1749
BARRINGER Margaret, on list of membs. 1870
BARTHOLOMEW John of Charterhouse
    m. Elizabeth Henton 1669
BARTON Thomas
    m. Mary
    dispute with Wm. Goodridge of Winthill 1693
    gift for poor Friends 1708
§ BASTIN Edward Philip, recovered from diphtheria 1862
§ BASTIN Charles Edward, listed 1879
BATT Anna of Street, d. Jasper b.1655 d.1689
    m. William Lawrence 1674
§ BATT William of Sidcot - Superintendent of SS. 1821-1839

§ BATT Mary wife of Wm.   d. 1835
    ch. Sarah m. Barton Dell 16-6-1835
        Mark
        Anna Maria
        Richard
        Phebe
BATTEN John of Banwell (a "common drunkard", test. against 1723)
    m. Martha Jennings of Banwell 1720
    Martha received money from John Jenkins' legacy 1728
BATTEN James of Banwell s. of John and Martha
    sent to school at Glaston 1735
BEACHAM Mary of Burrington
    m. William Lovell 1667
BEAR Anna "who sometime since lived in Axbridge" required cert. of
    clearness for marriage. 1721
§ BECK Alice, listed 1885.
BEESS Sarah of Burrington, a poor friend who reg. rec. charity money. d.1705?
    m. Richard Beess in Winscombe Church 1664 (nee Sarah Brodman)
BELL Caroline . Rec. into membs. 1856
BENNETT Hannah of Bristol
    m. William Jenkins of Sidcot 1699
§ BENTLY Ethel, listed 1900, at PM. 1905
BENTLY Elizabeth, moved to Penketh in 1903
§ BENWELL John. Moved to Sidcot 1784. First Superintendent of SS. 1808
    Clerk of MM.
    m. Martha (Overseer of Sidcot Mtg.)
BENWELL Sarah, d. John and Martha
    m. Robert Willmott of Pensford, at Sidcot 9-11-1804
BENWELL Hannah, d. John and Martha
    m. Arnee Frank of Bristol, at Sidcot 9-11-1805
BENWELL Mary, d. John and Martha
BENWELL Martha, d. John and Martha
BENWELL Lydia
    m. Thos. Trustlade Sparkes at Chew 19-1-1820
BENWELL Rebecca
BENWELL Joseph (s.John?)
    Moved to Bristol 1807, m. by priest 1808 then moved back.
    Disowned 1808.
BINNS Rachel of Sidcot (prev. Bristol)
    m. Edwin Miles of Poole, Saddler (bro. Joseph), at Sidcot 15-4-1828
BINNS Charles and wife, adm. to membs. of W-s-M mtg. 1864
    Charles made minister. 1867
BINNS Richard and Elizabeth of Coombehurst, Sidcot,
    1st mentioned 1895, moved away 1900.
    ch. Henry
        William Bryan
BISHOP Ann, on list of members 1830, d. sometime before 1846
BISHOP Maria, on Comm. for Summer School 1905.
BISHOP Charles a., listed 1907.
§ BLAKE Salome, listed 1897, rep. to MM. 1898, moved away 1902.
BLAKE Nona a. 1st listed 1901, joined by 1906.
BLOGG Thomas, needs cert. of removal 1900.

QUAKERS AT SIDCOT

BOARD Sarah of Winscombe
    m. Joseph Farmer 1706
BOBBET William. Convinced 1789. Moves to Bristol 1790
BOBBET Ann, of Churchill, widow of above, contributed to collection 1860.
    d. 31/10/66 aged 86, buried at Bristol.
BOBBETT Herbert J., of Churchill, moved into area 1892.
BOBBETT John Winter, Goathurst, Wins.. Listed 1910
    Emily
    ch. Florence Ada
BOWNAS Samuel (1676-1763), visited Sidcot.
§ BRACHER Anne Mary, adm. to membs. 1866, had been to Sidcot School.
§ BRADLEY Sarah, girls' First Class teacher,
    m.§ Basil P. Megahy, Science Teacher at SS. 1881-96
BRAGG Margaret, Oakridge, Sidcot. Listed 1906
BRAGG Susan Anna, Oakridge, Sidcot. Listed 1906
BRAYTON Patience. Visited Sidcot from Swansey, Massachusetts, 1784
    Set their slaves free 1758.
BRETELLE Ethel a. 1st listed 1899.
BREVETER Henrietta W, on list of membs. 1870.
    lived in Lausanne, Switzerland.
BREVETER Henrietta Theresa, on list of membs. 1870.
    d. Henrietta.
§ BRISON Sylvia E.. Listed 1916.
BROCK Ezekiell of Charterhouse. Poor and "ancient" friend 1710. d.1712
    m. Jane Plumly of Priddy, 1700, (lived together "in one hous" first)
BROCKBANK Amy, Sunnybrae, Winscombe
§ BROOKS David moved in, 1850. Moved to Christchurch 1851.
BROOKS Emma Kate, adm. into membs. 1893.
BROOKS Howard Lewis, Winscombe Post Master. Door Keeper 1902-1904.
§ BROWN Harriette, on staff 1874.
BROWN Charles and Mary, 1st entry on list 1893, mvd. to W-s-M 1894.
BROWN Adelaide, listed 1906
BRYAN Elizabeth Mary, 4 Jubilee Homes, Langford. Listed 1916.
BRYANT Alice. Appears to have been looked after by Sidcot friends 1776.
§ BUCK Mary Louisa, listed 1882
BURCHAM Charles and Mary, moved into Fairlie Lawn, Sidcot, 1890
BURCHAM Charles Henry, s. Charles and Mary
BURCHAM Gertrude Mary, on Comm. for social with her father, Charles 1896.
BURCHAM C. Lilian, d. Charles and Mary, moved away 1900.
BURCHAM Margaret Emily, d. Charles and Mary,
    on Comm. for Summer School, 1905.
BURCHAM George Alfred, s. Charles and Mary.
BURDGE Thomas of Winscombe
    m. Mary Slape of Glaston (by a priest, he not found to be clear) 1718
BURGESS David, on list of members 1830, moved by 1846
BURN Annie A., came to Sidcot 1902. Wife of R. Christie.
    Clerk to Sidcot Mtng. 1907-11 and 1917-20.
§ BURN R. Christie, SS. Senior Master 1902-29.
    Friend of Bevan Lean.
    Lived at Fairview, Sidcot

CAPPER Mary (1755-1845), visited Sidcot, 4th May 1800, from Birmingham.
CHAPPELL Edmund of Worle, Husbandman.
    Released from prison 1686 after 4 yrs.
    m. Dorcas Whiting 1678
CHAPPELL John of Worle, Husbandman. 9 yrs in prison, released 1686.
§ CHATFIELD Elizabeth, on Comm. for Summer School 1905.
    Appointed one of collectors for 1903.
CHURCHOUSE Thomas of Sidcot Mtg. Poor. Rec. money 1734.
CHURCHMAN John (1705-1775), visitor from America.
    Chester Co. Pennsylvania. A friend of John Woolman.
CLARE John of Frome
    m. Elizabeth Stoudley of Axbridge 1699
CLARK Mary Anna, The Coombe, d. A.T. and Mary Tanner
    m. out to Robert Clark, but not disowned, 1862
    Moved to Almondsbury 1893
§ CLARK Henry Robert, of Hillside, Sidcot. Art master of SS. 1881-1920
CLARK Mary Louisa, wife of Henry.
    ch. Ethel Mary
        Walter Henry
        Jessie
        Clifford Stanley
CLARK George E. listed 1885
§ CLARK Mary Jane, listed 1886
CLARK Robert William, The Coombe, Sidcot. 1st listed 1890.
    Moved to Vancouver with his wife, Alice and family 1892.
CLARK Alice, wife of Robert.
    ch. Robert Hamilton Bright
        Arthur Tanner
CLARK Alfred Sturge, of Sidcot, 1st listed 1893
CLARK Lilian Aubrey, of Sidcot, then Croydon, listed 1893
CLARK Theodora Elizabeth of Sidcot, listed 1893. In Egypt 1885.
    Ifield, nr. Crawley 1886
CLARK Margaret of Sidcot, listed 1896
    (All four above 1st listed at same address)
CLARK T. Beavan, on Comm. for Summer School 1905.
    Also on various other comms. Listed 1902
    Lived at Quarry Batch, Winscombe.
CLARK Margaret Eddington of Sidcot,
    m. Thomas Arnold Cash, not a member, at Sidcot 1904.
§ CLARK James, listed 1902
§ CLEGG Isabella a., listed 1914.
CLUTTON Winifred, Chateau de St. Angel, Aude, France. Listed 1915.
§ COCKIN Richard, at SS. 1822-23.
COLES Joyce a. 1st added to list 1891, too feeble to attend 1894.
COMER John of Cheddar
    reg. at MM. Sometimes at his house e.g. 1736.
    legacy of £100 left for poor friends.
    m. Sarah
§ COMPTON Theodore, moved into area 1859
    Artist, and author of 'A Mendip Valley'.

COMPTON Elizabeth, wife of above,
>ch. Edward Theodore
>>Marian Elizabeth
>>Louisa Matilda
>>William Cookworthy

COMPTON Edward Theodore, of Sidcot Lodge, and Feldafing Bavaria. Artist.
COMPTON Louisa, see above. Resigned 1878.
>But m. in Sidcot MH. to John R. Dutton 1905.

COLE Hannah Baker of Sidcot
>m. John Benwell Willmott of Congresbury ,miller, at Claverham 17-10-1838
>Double wedding with Sarah Willmott (J.B.'s sister) and Francis Osmond.
>Moved to Cardiff with infant son, Albert, 1840.

COLE Eliza of Woodborough
>m. Robert Willmott of Congresbury, shopkeeper, at Bath, 19-6-1840

COLLET Anthony (mentioned in connection with dispute between Wm. Jenkins and Webb Davis 1724).

COLLINS Martha. Poor friend. Rec. money 1790.

§ COOK Florence A.. Listed 1916.

COOMER James of Cheddar
>m. by priest
>d.1734 leaving legacy of #40 interest of which for repair of Sidcot MH

COOMER John (poss.same as John COMER above).
>rec. money from Wm. Reeve's legacy 1709.

COOPER Norman C. a. Strathmore, Wins.. Listed 1916.

CRAMP A. Winifred, Branstock, Shipham. Listed 1921

CRAY (or CROY) William of Sidcot. Poor and suffers from gout 1710. d.1713
>m. Susan Austin of Banwell. 1695

CRAY John bro. of Wm.. Poor. Rec. money from Wm. Reeve's legacy 1709.

CRAY John s. of Wm. and Susan
>"pd. Jno. Cray to pay for a shroud and coffin for his father
>>Wm. Cray 13s."

§ CROUCH John. Superintendent of SS. 1811-1812
>m. Margaret
>d. Margaret
>s. Richard Abell

CRUICKSHANK Edwin, Hillside Cottage, Wins.. 1919.
>Nora
>ch. Angus.

CUFFE Michael. Poor. Charity money distributed by Abrm. Thomas 1713.

CUFFE Mary, w.of Michael
>lived in Beluton MH.. Murdered 1727.

CURRY Sarah, formerly SEAMAN then SAY, reinstated into membs. 1861
>m. Josiah Curry. She never stopped attg. mtg. and brought their ch. up as Friends. Moved to Bristol.

CURTIS Thomas of Nempnet d.1752

CURTIS Mary of Nempnet w. of Thomas, left with large family.
>m. Thomas Vowles 1755

CURTIS Sarah d. of Mary and Thomas
>m. Thos. Tanner of Banwell, at Sidcot 8-5-1770

CURTIS Hannah d. of Mary and Thomas
>m. Wm. Tanner of Bleadon, at Sidcot 29-3-1771

CURTIS Mary Jnr. d. M. and T.
CURTIS Martha (d. M. and T.?)
    rec. charity money 1772.
    m. by priest to Joseph DERRICK 1777 but condemned her action.
    Lived at Max Mills.
CURTIS Thomas (s. M. and T.?) at MM. 1777
    m. by priest 1778.
CURTIS William (s. M. and T.?)
    m. by priest. Test. against 1774.

DAVIS Gabriel of Claverham, Yeoman. d. 1689
    m. Ann Yeales of Churchill 1677
    reg. at MM.
DAVIS Sarah of Sidcot
    m. Timothy Willis 1690
DAVIS (DAVESS) Joan of Rowberrow
    m. John Allen 1699
DAVIS Mary of Axbridge
    m. by priest 1704
DAVIS Gabriel s. Gabriel and Ann
    of age 1707, Richard and John Hipsley being guardians.
    m. Mary Sturges of Langford 1713
DAVIS Mary of Axbridge d. Gabriel and Ann
    guardians Richard and John Hipsley
    m. proposed to Saml. Chivers of Widcombe 1709
    but Saml. died before m. could take place.
    m. Wm. Herbert of Weymouth, distiller, 1711
DAVIS Webb, nephew of Wm. Jenkins. Had dispute with W.J. 1724
    m. Rachel Harris of County of Gloucester 1721
DAVIS Joanna of Banwell
    m. James White of Hutton 1742
§ DAVIS Amelia Ann, on list of membs. 1870.
    Girl's matron for 33 yrs. Left 1900.
DAY Mrs.! a. 1st listed 1890
§ DELL Barton of Sidcot
    m. Sarah Batt at Sidcot 16-6-1835
§ DELL John A., on Comm. for Summer School 1905
    Door keeper 1904.
DERRICK Martha, nee. Curtis
    m. by priest 1777 but continues to receive charity money.
    Applies for membership for her 6 children 1789 but not
        accepted "for the present".
DORY John of Butcombe, carpenter.   (Fit 1668)   d. 1696
    m. Frances   d. 1691
    reg. at MM.
DREWETT Jeffrey, Sidcot rep. 13/6/1866.
DUDLEY Mary (1750-1823) visited Sidcot 1798, from Bristol.
DURSTON Mrs.! a. 1st listed 1890.
DUTTON Louisa Mary, Wintrath, Wins.. Listed 1908.
    [m. John Rowe]
DYER Suzanna of Winthill
    m. James Fear 1770

QUAKERS AT SIDCOT

§ DYMOND Henry. Left on m.. Returned as Superintendent 1854-1865. A Minister.
  m.è Edith Frank at Bristol 1-10-1822
DYMOND Henry jnr. s. Henry and Edith
  Resigned, having fought in the Federal Army in the American Civil War.
§ DYMOND Josephina Sparks, sis. Henry Jnr.. Lived at Sidcot Lodge prior to m.
  Overseer 1859
  m. John Fry Wilkey 1862
DYMOND Miriam, d. Henry and Edith. Lived at Sidcot Lodge.
DYMOND Bertha, d. Henry and Edith
  m. Arthur Gregory at Sidcot, 5/5/1858
DYMOND Mary   d. 8/8/1865
DYMOND Frances   d. 20/9/1867 registered at Banwell

EAP John, servant to Sarah Comer of Cheddar.
EDDINGTON Arthur Henry B.A.(Lond.) 1st Friend graduate on the staff. 1866-?
§ EDMUNDS Doris, listed 1916
EDWARDS Maria, Caretaker of MH. for at least 12 yrs. until 1872.
ELDRIDGE Amy Margaret, [a], Clanville. Listed 1916.
ELIOTT Arnold and Beatrice, at Penscot, Shipham, 1919.
ELLIS James of Winscombe
  m. Sarah Naish of Claverham irregularly 1740. Test. against.
§ ELLIS John Dafforn and Elizabeth - Heads of SS. 1820-21.
  ch. Lewis Fry
      Rebecca Ellis
      Henry Ellis
ELLORY Laurence. Not supporting testimony against tythes 1705.
§ EVANS Josiah and Mary, Superintendents 1865/1873
  Josiah rec. a minister 1866.
  Left to become Superintendants of Ackworth, 1873.
EVANS Herbert John, s. Josiah and Mary b. 11/7/1861
EVANS Edith Mary , d. Josiah and Mary b. 14/11/1863
EVANS Arthur Rainsford, s. Josiah and Mary b. 25/3/1865
§ EVANS Gertrude Marian, d. Josiah and Mary, on list of membs. 1870
  Moved into School 1901
EVANS Charles Irwin, s. Josiah and Mary, on list of membs. 1870
  At St. John's College, Oxford. 1901
  On Comm. for Summer School 1905.
  m. Katherine Susan. Lived in Rose Cottage.
  ch. Michael I.
EVANS Fanny moved in, 1855
EVANS Mary, on list of membs. 1870
EVANS M. A. a., listed 1919.
EVANS S. a., listed 1909.
EVERED Eliza, nee SEAMAN
  m. in Church 1860.
  Disowned, altho' she said she still wished to att. mtgs.

FARMER John of Shipham or Winscombe
  m. Sarah
  Had rebellious daughters, 1699.
FARMER Joseph s. of John and Sarah
  m. Sarah Board of Winscombe 1706.

FARMER Judith d. of John and Sarah
    m. Thomas Addams of Clutton
FARRAND Isabella, rep. to MM. 10th mo. 1898. On Comm. for Summer School 1905.
    Lived at Penscot, Shipham. Moved to York by 1921.
FARRINGTON Walter Byford (not a member) d. 13/11/1865
FEAR James of Winthill and Loxton
    m. Susanna Dyer of Winthill at Sidcot, 27-3-1771
    Absents himself from Mtg.. Test. against 1782.
FEAR Susanna needs charity money regularly.
FEAR John of Loxton, s. James and Susanna   d. 29-11-1841
    m. Lydia Tanner, d. Thomas and Sarah of Winthill, 1800
FEAR Lydia, same as above, on list to rec. charity money for many
    years. d. 30/3.1853
FEAR Eliza d. John and Lydia - disowned for not attending mtgs.
    d.10/5/1863; buried at Sidcot.
FEAR John jnr. s. John and Lydia - disowned for immoral conduct.
FEAR Louisa d. John and Lydia - on list of members 1830, moved by 1846.
FEAR Lydia jnr. d. John and Lydia - on list of members 1830, moved by 1846.
FELL James of Glastonbury, schoolmaster.
    m. Grace Thomas, d. of Abram. and Grace of Banwell.
FERRIS Thomas, schoolmaster in Woodborough.
    Clerk of M.M. 1834 - 1840
FERRIS Maria wife of Thomas
    ch. Maria jnr.
       Thomas Francis
       Eliza
       Matilda
       Henry
FERRIS Elizabeth, on list to rec. charity money for many years, in the
    1830's and 40's. d.12/11/1855
§ FERRIS Eliza, (see above) took on job of looking after girls straight after her
    apprenticeship. 1846
    m. Henry Barron Smith at W-s-M, 2/7/1856
FERRIS Matilda, (see above), still on list of membs. 1870
FERRIS Henry of Beech House, Churchill, (see above), on list of membs. 1875
    m. Ellen
    ch. Ellen
       Elizabeth
       Grace
       Henry
       Hugh
    Moved in 1886.
FERRIS Elizabeth (see above ?) Upover, Shipham. Listed 1916.
FLOWER Mary, convinced 1779.
    (Claverham or Sidcot)
FOLLETT Thomas of South Brent, miller. d. 12/11/1856
    m. Mary (both moved into area 1813), Mary d.1844
FOLLETT Mary d. Mary and Thomas
FOLLETT Rouckliffe s. Mary and Thomas. Miller of South Brent
    m. Mary Kidd of Bristol   d. 1872
FOLLETT Jane d. Mary and Thomas
FOLLETT Fanny d. Mary and Thomas - on list of members 1830, moved by 1846

QUAKERS AT SIDCOT

FOLLETT Abraham s. Mary and Thomas - on list of members 1830, d. by 1846
FOLLETT John s. Mary and Thomas - on list of members 1830, moved by 1846

FOLLETT Thomas jnr. s. Mary and Thomas - on list of members 1830
    m. by priest 1856
FOLLOWS Ruth, (1717-1808) visitor from Weston, Notts., 1773 and 1784.
    Visited most of the Mtgs. in England.
FOTHERGILL John (1676-1744), from Yorkshire, visited Sidcot 1733
§ FOTHERGILL Samuel, 1841-1845.
§ FOULDEN John. Moved to Sidcot 1924. Moved to Bristol 1927.
    m. Ann Wheeler at Sidcot 5-7-1831
§ FOWLER Dora L. listed 1919.
§ FOX Margaret, listed 1906.
FOX Amy C. a., listed 1908.
FRAMPTON William of Axbridge, MM. reg. held at his house.
    m. Sarah Mocket of Axbridge 1729
FRAMPTON Mary, mentioned in mins. of women's MM. 1756.
FRANK Arnee of Bristol, Ironmonger, s. Thomas and Elizabeth.
    m. Hannah Benwell, at Sidcot 5-4-1805
§ FRANK Edith, d. Arnee and Hannah, moved to Sidcot 1820-21
    m. Henry Dymond
    Ret. to Sidcot in 1854 as headmistress
§ FRANK Ann and John s. Arnee and Hannah, move in, 1847
    Superintendents of SS.
    John Frank rec. minister 1874
    moved out, 1852.
FRANKS Martha E. a. 1st listed 1901.
FREEMAN William, reinstated 9th mo. 1852
FRY Hannah of Banwell
    m. Francis Palmer 1678
FRY Mary of Banwell
    m. Edmond Jennings 1685
FRY William, one of Sidcot Reps. 12-3-45
    moved out 12th mo. 1847
FRY Albert, on list of membs. 1870
FRY Richenda, d. 13/2/1872
    Albert Magnus, on list of membs. 1870
    Richenda Mary, on list of membs. 1870
    George Talema, on list of membs. 1870
§ FRY Constance Emily, listed 1897, moved away 1898.
FULLER James Cannings of Sidcot, moved into area 1821, went with son Robert Charlton to America for a few months, required cert. 3rd mo. 1833. Moved to New York with wife and family 1834
FULLER Lydia wife of James C.
    ch. Robert Charlton
        Samuel
        John Wilkinson
        James
        Bonville
        Sumner
        Hannah

GARDNER Jane of Axbridge
   m. George Hardidge of Sidcot 1714/15
§ GAYNOR Elsie C. listed 1919.
GIBSON Elizabeth a. 1st listed 1901
§ GILKES Benjamin Gilbert and Ann, moved into SS. as Heads 1838.
   ch. Miriam
       Caroline, d.1844
       Resigned from SS. 1846, moved away from area 1851
GILKES Emma. Moved into the area 1838
§ GILPIN Joseph Sturge,
   m. Rachel Lislie of Wells in Norfolk, 1854.
GOODRIDGE William of Winthill, Yeoman. d.1706
   m. Margaret Gundry of Street, d.1710
   often at MM.
GORDON-FORBES Elizabeth Lucy, Lewisham, Wins..
   [m. Meredith Percy]
   ch. Ian Percival
       Jasmine
§ GOUDGE Frederic A. listed 1903
GOUGH Agnes a., Oakridge, listed 1918.
GOUCH Benjamin, at SS. in 1857 during the diphtheria epidemic, when he
   amused the boys by reciting 'Oliver Twist' from memory.
§ GRAHAM Lydia S. Listed 1911.
§ GRAHAM A. Margaret. Listed 1913.
GREEN James, lived in London 1709 but had previously
   lived with Wm. Lovell.
GREENFIELD Lydia, on list of membs. 1870
GREGORY Hannah - on list of members 1830
   Sidcot Overseer 1845; d. 1866 aged 86.
§ GREGORY Lydia, S. Schoolmistress 1812-20
§ GREGORY Robert, S. Superintendent 1812-17 (d. in 1817)
§ GREGORY Margaret of Street, apprentice on the girl's side, d. 1851.
§ GREGORY Arthur m. Bertha Dymond at Sidcot 5/5/1858
GREGORY Isabella, on list of members 1870
GREGORY Louisa C., lived at C. Brown's 1893-94.
GREGORY Elizabeth, The Meadow Cottage, listed 1910
GRIFFITH John (1713-1776) visited Sidcot, from Darby Pennsylvania.
   Was captured by pirates on his way over.
GRIGG Prudence, moved back into Banwell 1798. Sidcot overseer.
   w. William
GRIGG Mary, d. of Prudence
   m. John Sanders of Bristol at Sidcot 31-5-1811
GRIGG John Horsington, cabinet maker, s. of Prudence.
   apprenticed in Bristol 1801, in trouble for drinking 1808.
   m. Betty
GRIGG Sarah, d. of Prudence
GRIGG Charles, s. of Betty and John H. b.1821
GRIGG Mary, d. of Betty and John H. b.1823
GRIGG Betsy rec. charity money 1830-
   wife of John (not a member) app. for memb. for her ch. William,
   Prudence, Thomas and Charles, but not accepted, 1822. d. 1853.

QUAKERS AT SIDCOT

GRUBB John, The Down, (now known as Queensmead Court) Wins.. Listed 1901.
    Clerk 1902-1906, and in 1924.
GRUBB Madeline, wife of John, on Comm. for Summer School 1905. Tel. 19
GRUBB Helen, d. John and Madeline.
    m. John E. Hall of Leeds, 1904.
GRUBB Gertrude a., listed 1910.
GRUBB Anne at Mendip View. Listed 1916
GRUBB Erica, elderly member in 1940
§ GRUBB Isabel, listed 1921

HALLAM Edward, Axbridge chemist, and keen botanist. d.1867.
    m. Elizabeth 2/12/1875
HALLAM Eliza Stott moved to Bristol 1851
HALLAM Elizabeth of Axbridge, on list of membs. 1870
HALLIDAY Elizabeth and Susannah a., listed 1920.
HANKINSON Jessie, a. listed 1907
HARDIDGE George of Sidcot
    m. Jane Gardner of Axbridge 1715
    test. against for frequent drunkenness 1721
    Jane Hardidge and children sick. need relief 1726
    moved to Sidcot MH. 1729
    daughter needs place 1730
HARDIDGE George s. George and Jane b. 1722
HARDIDGE William s. George and Jane b. 1723
    both sent to school 1732 then apprenticed in Bath
    both ran away.
§ HARRIS J. Theodore, listed 1889.
§ HARROD James Tyler, listed 1903
HATCH William of Allerton att. at Sidcot, applies for membership 1803
    but rejected. Died, a member, 1822 aged 81.
HATTERSLEY Thomas, on list of members 1830, d. before 1846.
HARWOOD Edward of Bristol
    m. Mary Tanner d. Rachel and Wm. at Sidcot 27-10-1770
HAWKINS Ann, mentioned in mins. of women's MM. 1760.
HAWKINS William (+2) a. 1st listed 1890.
HAYLES Ada at Newcombe, Sidcot, listed 1916
§ HEALD Thomas Dann, listed 1901
HEATH John. At MM. 1806 as rep. for Sidcot, moved to Bristol 1807.
HEATH Florence, listed 1906.
HEATH Lilian, Trelawney House, Axbridge. Listed 1911.
HEATH Ada Louisa, Wayside, Wins. 1918.
HEDLEY Beatrice a. 1st listed 1899.
HEMMENS James and Hannah, took care of MH. 1873-1875.
HIGGINS William, servant at S.S., add. into membs. 1818. Moved away 1825.
    Returned. d. 31/7/1867.
HIGGINS Eliza, wife of William (?), put in charge of overseeing the heating and
    cleaning of the M.H. 1872.
HILL William a. 1st listed 1901.
HIPPISLEY Mary of Churchill
    mother of Ann Yeales (and John and Richard Hipsley ?)

HIPSLEY Richard of Stock in Parish of Churchill, Yeoman. d. 1738
    m. Hannah Tucker of Butcombe 1696. d. 1709
    reg. at MM. Sidcot overseer.
HIPSLEY John of Chew Magna, cordwainer, fuller.
    m. Mary d. 1671
    v. reg. at MM. sev. times at his house.
HIPSLEY Mary d. Hannah and Richard.
    m. James Wreach of Congresbury, at Sidcot, 1721
HIPSLEY Hannah d. Hannah and Richard, b.1700
    m. Richard Thomas of Portishead, at Sidcot, 1726
HIPSLEY Richard of Stock, yeoman, s. Hannah and Richard. b.1708 d.1767
    Minister, Overseer of Sidcot mtg.,
    at MM. reg. 1730-
    m. Ann Salter d. of James Salter of Puddimore. d.1779
HIPSLEY John s. Hannah and Richard, b.1703
    m. Mary Thomas of Wrington, at Claverham, 1733
HIPSLEY Ann d. Hannah and Richard b.1701
HIPSLEY Sarah d. Hannah and Richard b.1705
HIPSLEY Ann of Shiplett
HIPSLEY Sarah of Shiplett. d. Ann
    m. by priest to Richard Amesbury of Shiplett 1739.
    Test. against. 1739.
HIPSLEY Samuel of Shiplett, s. Ann
    m. by priest and test. against 1745
    reinstated 1748
HIPSLEY Mary d. Ann and Richard b. 25-1-1740
    At momen's MM. 1761
    m. William Phippen of Bristol at Sidcot 6-12-1764
HIPSLEY John s. Ann and Richard b. 21-2-1741
    m. Elizabeth Selfe 1762
    Moved, with his family, to Ackworth School in 1790
    where he became superintendent.
HIPSLEY Richard of Stock, s. Ann and Richard b.19-8-1742 d.19-5-1820 aged 77.
    m. Betty Palmer, his 1st cousin, by priest 1784, disowned.
    Betty and Richard successfully applied to be re-admitted into
    membership 1813, and then received charity money.
    Betty d. 8-2-1820 aged 76.
HIPSLEY Ann d. Ann and Richard b. 26-2-1744 d. as a child
HIPSLEY Ann d. Ann and Richard b. 9-6-1746 d. 1802
HIPSLEY Samuel s. Ann and Richard
    m. Lydia Jeffries of Melksham 1771 and moves to Melksham.
HIPSLEY Robert and James, twins, b.14th July 1753 d.Oct. 1753
HIPSLEY Richard s. Betty and Richard of Stock
    applied for membership as son of disowned parents 1803
    not accepted but care of friends required.
    Applied again 1808. Disowned for immoral conduct, 1814.
    d. (not a member) at Lower Langford 1/9/1862
HIPSLEY Mary Ann, a minor, app. for memb. 1837. Admitted.
    Went to meeting with her parents who were former members.
    Disowned for immoral conduct 1844.
HOBBS Samuel
    belonged to Sidcot Mtg. moved 1745

QUAKERS AT SIDCOT

HOBBS Richard
    rec. from legacy 1751
HOLDEN Doris a., listed 1920.
HOLDER Robert of Westbury-sub-Mendip
    does't support test. against tythes 1705
    proposed m. to Hester Sam of Street 1711
    but went off the idea 1712
HORSINGTON John of Locking, farmer
    m. Mary
HORSINGTON Prudence d. John and Mary
    m. William Grigg of Bristol, cabinet maker, at Sidcot, 1783
HORSINGTON Caroline a., listed 1919.
HUCKER John of Worle, poor, rec. #1 from Wm. Reeve's legacy 1709
HUCKER Mary of Worle, w. of John, rec. 10s from John Chappel's legacy 1712
    in dept. 1713. Hip bone set 1717.
HUCKER Grace d. John and Mary, sent to London to John Whiting Jnr. 1713
HUGHES Stephen Jarret moved into Sidcot area 1823, left 1825
HULL Henry (1765-1834) visited Sidcot, from Stamford, New York State.
HUNT Ann "now residing in vicinity of Sidcot Meeting"
    m. James Player of Portishead at Claverham, 1756
HUNT Sarah, moved in from S. Wales 1842
    Disowned for marrying out 1845
HUTCHINSON Herbert, Coombehurst, Wins. listed 1918
    Elisabeth
    ch. George Woods
       Herbert Procter
       Jonathan
       Christopher West
       Margaret Massey
       Hugh Bernard
       Alice Mary
       Elizabeth Rachel
HUTCHINSON Elizabeth Bateman, Hillside Cottage, Wins.. listed 1919.

§ JACKSON Hugo H., listed 1913.
JACOBS John Reuben a. listed 1896, left Sidcot prob. 1898
JEFFREY William D., MM. rep. 6th. mo. 1866.
JEFFREY John F., Redcroft Cottages, Redhill, Wrington, Som..
    Emily
    ch. Mary Bell.
JEFFRIS Robert rec. charity money by Abraham Thomas, 1717-
JENKINS William of Hertford, Sidcot Schoolmaster
    dispute with MM. 1717/18
       m. Hannah Bennet of Bristol 1699
JENKINS John of Keynsham then Axbridge   d. 1728
    m. Anna Laurence, widdow, of Axbridge   d. 1729
JENNINGS Edmond of Corston and Banwell
    poor, rec. from legacy 1691
    m. Mary Fry of Banwell 1685
JENNINGS Mary (w. Edmond), rec. from Wm. Lawrence's will.
JENNINGS Martha of Banwell, d. Edmond and Mary
    m. John Batten at Sidcot 1720

JOHN Margaret adm. to membs. 12/3/1856
§ JONES Elizabeth K., listed 1918.
JONES Florence, [Paul Edwards], Sidcot. Listed 1919.

§ KEATLY Hilda M., listed 1919.
KENWAY Gawen, apptd. Deputy Clerk, 1902
KENWAY Elizabeth Lucy, wife of above
    on Comm. for Summer School 1905.
    Lived at Mendip View, Wins..
KENWAY Hannah, Lewisham, Wins. listed 1910.
KING John, and family, rec. charity money 1759
    moved to Butley 1770
KING Elizabeth, wife of John?, rec. 6s from Women's MM. 1760.
KING Elsie, a. listed 1907.
KING Phebe Ann, Sunnybrae, Wins. listed 1908
§ KITCHING William,
    m. è Louisa Wilmot, at W-s-M, 1862, grandparents of
        Wilfred Kitching, General of the Salvation Army.
§ KITCHING Mabel, on Comm. for Summer School 1905.
§ KNIGHT Francis Arnold, author and schoolmaster,
    eventually lived at Wintrath
    m. è Jane Redfern at Stockport 24/6/1875.
    Wrote 'The Heart of the Mendip' etc.
    'A History of Sidcot School' in 1908. d. 1915.
KNIGHT Jane, wife of Francis, on Comm. for Summer School 1905, Tel. 9.
§ KNIGHT Louisa Mary, d. Francis and Jane, at Ackworth School 1898
    m. John R. Dutton, 1905.
KNIGHT Sarah Matthews (w. Henry) of Wintrath, listed 1898.
§ KNIGHT Dorothy, on Comm. for Summer School 1905.
KNOWLES Alice Mary, Quarry Batch, listed 1921.

LANCASTER George a., listed 1816.
LANCASTER Florence, Sidcot. Listed 1913.
§ LANE Joseph, 2nd in command when Francis Knight was 1st master.
    Became School Secretary, and served the School for 34 yrs.
    Gave the first singing lessons.
    P.M. Clerk 1886-1902
LANE Lucy, wife of Joseph, MM. Rep. 9th mo. 1883.
    ch. Joseph John
        Arthur Samuel
        Benjamin Harold
LANE Annie, Moss Cottage, Wins.. Listed 1916
LANEY Lydia of Banwell, on list of membs. 1874.
LANSDOWNE, George Bevil Alexander and Helen Anstice
    ch. Hazel Mary Joy
    Lower Winterhead Farm, listed 1921.
LA TROBE Mrs. and daughter, a. 1st listed 1899
LAWRENCE William of Axbridge, draper. Fit. 1668 d.1697
    In prison for 9 mo. 1682
    m.1 Mary Dean of Barrow in Kingsbury, 1671 d.1672
    m.2 Anna Batt of Street, 1674 d.1689
    m.3 Agnes Wilson, 1691
    reg. at MM. sev. times at his house

QUAKERS AT SIDCOT

LAWRENCE Edith of Axbridge, widow   d.1691
    legacy to friends.
LAWRENCE Sarah of Axbridge d. Wm.
    m. John Whitehead 1696
LAWRENCE Anna of Axbridge, widow.
    m. John Jenkins of Keynsham 1705
§ LAWRENCE John, became professor of English Lit. at Tokio Univ.
    Membs. of Soc. accepted 14/2/1872
    Founder member of Sidcot O.S. Association.
§ LAWRENCE Henry, a junior teacher 1874-1881.
    Took M.A. at London Univ.. d. young.
LEAKER Emily Beatrice, Fairview, Sidcot. Listed 1916.
§ LEAN Bevan, Head of SS. from 1902-30, Tel. 2.
§ LEAN Mabel, a. wife of Bevan, b.1865 d.1948
    ch. a. Oscar and Owen.
LEE John, Clevedon House, Wins.. Listed 1916.
§ LEES Henry, on list of Sidcot reps. 9th mo. 1852.
    Apptd. Clerk to the Mtng. 1852.
§ LESLIE Adelaide, sn. Matron, took over in 1863 as Mistress when
    Edith Dymond was ill.
LEWIS Mary, d. 11/8/1867 registered at Banwell.
LEWIS Maud Vivian Julia (not a member) d. 26/11/1875
LEWIS Mary of Woodborough, listed 1886, MM. rep. 1888
LEWIS John, husb. of above, and d. Ada, admitted to membs. 1893.
LEWIS Isabel a. 1st listed 1890
LEWIS Annie a. 1st listed 1896 (left Sidcot, prob. 1898.)
LEWIS Ada Margaret, on Comm. for Summer School 1905. Lived at Lewisham, Wins..
LEWIS Gertrude Elizabeth, lived at Lewisham, Wins.. 1919.
§ LIDBETTER Martin, apprenticed to SS. 1834, Head of SS. 1852-53
    m. Elizabeth Serjeant of W-s-M at Sidcot 22-11-1843
    ch. Elizabeth Lucy b.9th mo. 1844
        Robert Martin
        Arthur Edward
§ LIDBETTER Robert M. (see above) on list of membs. 1870
    Apptd. Clerk 1871, as John Sharp moved.

§ LIDBETTER Deborah E. Listed 1910
§ LINNEY George Frederick, Jun., listed 1897
LINNEY Sarah Anne, w. Charles. Ivydene, Churchill. Listed 1910
    Mved. to Sandford View, Lynch, Wins..
    Laura Ethelwyn
    Francis Stewart
    Muriel Hudson
LINTERN William a. 1st listed 1893
LLOYD Margaret Louisa, Branstock, Shipham, listed 1921
    ch. HALLIDAY Elizabeth
        HALLIDAY Susanna
        HALLIDAY John
        HALLIDAY David
LOVELL John of Langford, tanner   d.1699
    m. Hannah   d.1680
    reg. at MM.

LOVELL Hannah d. Hannah and John of Langford
    m. Matthew Perrin of Taunton 1680
LOVELL John of Burrington and Langford, tanner, s. Hannah and John
    m. Mary Wallis, 1681   d.1699
LOVELL William of Havyatt in Wrington
    m. Mary Beacham 1667
    reg. at MM. Sidcot overseer
LOVELL John s. Mary and Wm.   d.1671
    Inclined to marry "one of the world"
    but m. Ann Harris of Bristol 1701
LOVELL Mary d. Mary and Wm.
    m. William Packer of Bristol 1714
LOVELL Ann, w. of John of Wrington
    Had large stone erected at husband's grave
    which had to be removed 1728.
LYNE Robert of Nempnett (Burrington)
    Disorderly 1668
    Goods distrained 1683

MACMILLAN Annie a. listed 1986 but left the neighbourhood 1898/9
MACHIN Ann of Sidcot add. to membs. 1848
MACSHANE Arthur a., listed 1908.
§ MALTBY Samuel. E. a. listed 1901
    m. 1. Marjorie, d. 1917. 3 ch. John, Catherine and Diana Mary.
    m. 2. Katherine Alexander in 1922 who died a few yrs. later.
    Left Sidcot to become Head of Penketh School.
MANFIELD Richard of Stock and Congresbury (Iwood)
    m. Mary Manning of Axbridge 1742
    reg. rec. charity money, looked after Richard Yeepe when ill, 1747
MANNING Joseph of Winthill
    m. Christian Nippery
    rec. from John Chappell's legacy 1711
    family rec. reg. 1711-
    rec. 10s because of great illness 1715
    house falls down 1721
MANNING Mary of Axbridge (d. Christian and Joseph?)
    m. Richd. Manfield 1742
MANNING William of Banwell s. Christian and Joseph
    m. Hannah Hales of Nailsea at Sidcot 1742
MANNING Christian (d. Christian and Joseph?) of Claverham Mtg.
    m. by priest 1749
MARRIAGE Caroline, Lostwood, Langford. 1919.
MARSHALL Francis, rec. charity money 1762
MASON Emma admitted to membs. 1852. She was brought up by Hannah C. Price.
MAW Catherine of Elmside, Sidcot, reinstated in 1892, MM. rep. 1893.
MAW Martha Maria of Elmside,
    reinstated 1896, having resigned about 30yrs. before
MAY Fannie E., R/he, Wins. listed 1910.
    Moved to St. Vincent, Cheddar.
§ MEGAHY Basil P., listed 1885
    m. § Sarah Bradley

QUAKERS AT SIDCOT

MELLUISH Thomas of Taunton
    acc. John Thomas of Sidcot on religious journeys 1790 etc.
MERREFIELD Roger
    reg. at MM. 1785-
    moved to Portishead 1788
    m. Mary Bewsey of Bristol
MERRYWEATHER Maria, The Firs, Churchill, listed 1898.
MIHILL Charles W. at Alfred Clarke's, The Meadow Cottage, Wins.
MILES Robert, of Chewton Mendip, on list of members 1830. d. by 1846.
MILES Martha, on list of members 1830.
MILES Joseph, of Winterhead, farmer.
    m. Elizabeth Binns of Bristol, at Bristol, Friars M.H., 9-10-1827
MILES Elizabeth, wife of above. d. 3/2/68
MILES Thomas Binns, s. of above
    m. Margaret Clark by priest, disowned 1853.
    Both reinstated 1855.
    ch. Charles Joseph d. 25/2/1855 aged about 7 mo..
        Margaret Elizabeth b. 17/1/1856
        Annie Clark b. 5/5/1857
    Both resigned 1872.
MILES Emma, d. Elizabeth and Joseph
    m. Joseph A. Petvin at Sidcot 15/4/1863
MILES Edwin, Sidcot rep. 1863, d. 1864
MILES Henry, enlists in army and disowned 1865
MILLER William Frederick of Summerfield, Sidcot, MM. rep. 1893.
    m. Mary M., MM. rep. 1892.
    Moved to Sunnybrae
MILLER J. a., listed 1909.
§ MILLWARD Rose, a. listed 1885. d. 1896.
MITCHELL Edith of Burrington, in prison 1658
MITCHELL John of Axbridge
MITCHELL John s. John of Axbridge
    m. Mary James of Paulton 1709
MOCKETT Sarah of Axbridge
    m. Wm. Frampton 1729
MOORE Henry of Burnham and Backwell, yeoman, b.1619 d.1685
    m.1 Mary Rogers 1645
    m.2 Mary Gundry 1658   d.1661
    m.3 Rachel Jobbins 1661   d.1685
§ MOORE Elizabeth, served as Mistress with Martin Lidbetter
    because his wife was delicate, 1852.
MORRIS Emma Matilda, on list of membs. 1830, moved by 1846.
§ MOSS Harriet J. listed 1875
§ MOSS Sophia, listed 1884
§ MURPHY Muriel E., listed 1921

NAISH Joseph, prominent Claverham Friend, shopkeeper
    lived in Congresbury and stood in as Head of Sidcot School 1817.
        Friend of John Benwell
NEWBERRY Edgar a., listed 1907.
NEWMAN Josiah a., Downfield, Wins..

NEWMAN Sarah Knight a., listed 1917.
  E. Winifred a..
NEWTH Constance [Charles], 5, South Hill, Sandford. 1919.
NICHOLLS Walter T., Parklands Mead, Sidcot. Listed 1913.
  Phyllis Constance.
§ NICKALLS Ada, listed 1897, moved away 1901.
NIPPER Mary, (wife of Wm.?), on list of membs. 1870.
NIPPER William, d. 15/5/1873 at Shipham,(not a memb.)
NORRIS Thomas of Banwell and Cleeve
  m. Jane Thetcher of Burrington (at Claverham?) 1723
  reg. at MM. rec. charity money 1772
NYE George, house in Woodborough mentioned 1706.

OLIVER Matilda a. 1st listed 1894
ORCHARD Joseph, rec. charity money 1756
OSMOND John, rec. charity money 1771
OSMOND Hannah, at Mrs Day's, West Street, Axbridge, listed 1876

PAGE Lucy a., listed 1919.
PAGEWOOD Gladys a., listed 1920.
PAGEWOOD Margaret, The School House, listed 1921
PALMER Francis of Compton Bishop
  m. Hannah Fry of Banwell 1678
PALMER James, resident in Sidcot area for a while 1784
PALMER William, on list of membs. 1830, moved by 1846. d. 14/6/1848
§ PALMER Elizabeth, listed 1891, moved away 1899.
PARKER Mary, on list of membs. 1830, d. by 1846.
PARKER Philip, almost certainly the last member of Chew Magna mtg.. d. 1856.
PARMITER Lavington and Sarah, moved into Sidcot area 1828,
  moved to Portishead before 1846.
PARSLEY Richard,
  gave land for MH. at Weston-s-Mare 1844
PARSONS William of Churchill, yeoman
  m. Sarah Bullock 1674   d.1675
  Lived with servant 1686
  Paid tythe but regretted it.
§ PATCHING Marjorie, listed 1910.
§ PAVEY Gertrude a., listed 1917.
PAYNE John, m. Elisabeth Amesbury at Sidcot 26-5-1761
PEARCE George of Winscombe, goods distrained 1679
PEARSON Edith P. c/o J. Grubb, The Down, Wins.. Listed 1906.
PEAT Ann, on list of membs. 1870.
PETSZEKE Margaret a., listed 1912.
§ PERKINS Hugh T. listed 1876.
PERRIN Matthew of Taunton, merchant,   d.1696
  m. Hannah Lovell of Langford 1680
  Legacy left for Friends
PETVIN Joseph Arthur,
  m. Emma Miles at Sidcot 15/4/1863
PHELPS Mary of Burrington, poor
  m. by priest 1688
PHELPS James of Burrington

QUAKERS AT SIDCOT

PHIPPEN William of Bristol
    m. Mary Hipsley of Stock at Sidcot 6-12-1764
§ PICKARD Lilian, MM. rep. 5th mo. 1899. Moved away 1901.
§ PITMAN Jane, otherwise known as Jenny, on list of membs. 1830.
    Overseer of Sidcot mtg., SS. Housekeeper. d. 12/3/1860.
PITMAN Rebecca, (born Strode) on list of membs. 1830.
    and on list for 1870.
PITMAN Solomon of Shipham, adm. to membs. 1872, having att. mtg. about 50 yrs.
    (Husband of above?)
    ch. Rebecca.
PITSTOW Isaac, staymaker, of Frome and Bath
    at Wm. Jenkin's school then apprenticed in Bath 1720
    m. Mary Stretch 1796
    reg. at MM. 1740-
PLAISTER Mary of Chuchill, re-admitted 1784
PLUMLY James of Priddy, labourer   d.1712
    m.1 Ann Smith of Cheddar 1681   d.1707
    m.2 Mary Astor of Chew 1709
PLUMLY John of Priddy, labourer   d.1700
    m. Ann
PLUMLY George of Priddy, labourer
    goods distrained 1670
PLUMLY Jane of Priddy
    m. Ezekiell Brock 1700
PLUMLY Richard of Westhay, poor man 1705
    advised to move nearer a meeting
PLUMMER Mary of Burrington
    m. Peter Walker 1673
POW Mary, given charity money reg. (by Sarah Thomas in 1757).
POWELL John B. a Sidcot rep. 12/9/49
PRICE Hannah C. of Oakridge
    Rec. as a minister. 1847
§ PRIEST Henry. W. listed 1915.
§ PRIESTMAN Florence Dent, listed 1911.
PUDNEY Robert Leaper, Westlands, Wins. listed 1906,
    m. Elizabeth Jane
    ch. Robert William Edward
        Elizabeth Allen
        Annie Benbow
    Moved to Auckland, New Zealand, before 1910.
§ PUMPHREY Maria, in charge of girls, 1847.
PUMPHREY Priscilla Hannah, MM. rep. 1888
PUMPHREY Samuel Baker of Springfield, Churchill, on SS. Comm. 1891,
    Husband of above
    MM. rep. 4th mo. 1888
    Moved to Summerfield Wins..
PUMPHREY Mary, d. Priscilla and Samuel. On Comm. for Peace set up in 1898

RADFORD Joseph of Axbridge, attender at Sidcot,
    applied for membership 1804, rejected,
    tries again 1809, rejected again.
§ RAWLINGS Hannah, listed 1881.

QUAKERS AT SIDCOT

§ RAWLINGS Henry, listed 1881.
READ Ann, on list of membs. 1830.
    Admitted into memb. 1833, having attended meeting for many years.
READ James, d. 18/2/1871 reg. at Axbridge (not a memb.).
§ REDFERN Jane, appointed 1872, transformed the girl's side in Josiah Evans time.
READ Nancy d. at Axbridge 8/5/1871
READ Clara, a. for 1 yr 1899-1900
REEVE William of Woodborough, s. of Thomas, baptised 1605.   d.1691
    m. Sarah
    qu. reg. at MM.
REEVE William Jnr. of Woodborough Green, husbandman,
    s. of Sarah and Wm.   d.1707
    m. Mary Willis 1688   d.1718
  reg. at MM. sev. times at his house
  left legacy to Friends
REEVE Mary w. of Wm.
    moved to Rowberrow after death of her husband
REEVE Thomas of Woodborough, s. of Sarah and Wm., baptised 1668
    m. Ann White 1699
  Ann Reeves' ministry unacceptable to Sidcot Friends 1703
  moved to Weymouth 1704
REEVES Annie, Buckhurst Hill, Essex. Listed 1911.
§ REYNOLDS Lucy, listed 1897
REYNOLDS Joan B., Craigside, Wins.. 1919.
RHODES Thomas, MM. rep. 12th mo. 1865.
RIDLER Selina, 2, Jubilee Homes, Langford. Listed 1915.
RICKETS Mary of The Lynch, Woodborough, listed 1876
    Moved to J. Lewis's
ROBINSON Elizabeth of Sidcot
    m. Emanuel Howitt of Farnsfield, Notts. at Sidcot 10-9-1846
§ ROBINSON Amy, listed 1885
§ ROBINSON Bertha, listed 1885
§ ROBSON Thomas, listed 1899-1900, and from 1915, in Sidcot Lodge.
ROBSON Ether a., The Home, Wins., listed 1918.
§ ROSE Elsie M., listed 1921
ROWLANDS Charles [Constance], Winscombe, listed 1921
§ ROWNTREE Walter Smithson, listed 1882
§ ROWNTREE Charles, listed 1892.
RUMNEY Elizabeth of Bristol and Sidcot
    m. Thomas Fry of Cullompton, Devon 1706

§ SALOME Anna Eliza, d.1853, registered at Cheddar.
SANDERS John of Bristol, grocer and cheesefactor
    m. Mary Grigg of Banwell 31-5-1811
§ SATTERTHWAITE Frederick, listed 1892, moved away 1901.
SAUNDERS Martin of Brislington and Banwell
    disorderly m. at Sidcot with Sarah Saunders 1692
    "too familiar with his maid servant" 1704
    test. against 1692 and 1704
SAVILLE Hannah M., 6, South Hill, Sandford. Listed 1915.
SAYER Samuel of Banwell and Worle, yeoman.   d.1682 in Prison
    m. Mary   d.1705

QUAKERS AT SIDCOT

SAYER Judith of Worle
    m. by priest 1701, test. against
SAYER Joseph of Banwell, admonished 1705
SEAMAN Samuel Hipsley moves into Sidcot area 1800
    m. contrary to rules and disowned 1805
    reinstated 1815 d. 3/9/1856
SEAMAN Sarah, wife of above.
SEAMAN Samuel, s. Samuel and Sarah.
    Disowned for the 'objectional character' of his ministry, in meeting for worship, 1842.
SEAMAN Edwin, s. Samuel and Sarah.
    First add. into membs. with the rest of the ch. 1818.
SEAMAN Sarah Hipsley, d. Samuel and Sarah
SEAMAN Robert, s. Samuel and Sarah.
    Disowned for non-attendance at meeting. 1836.
SEAMAN Eliza, d. Samuel and Sarah.
    Wished to resign 1842 but changed her mind.
SEAMAN Abraham, s. Samuel and Sarah.
    Resiged 1841
SEAMAN Alfred, s. Samuel and Sarah.
    Disowned for '...drinking to excess, profane swearing and other disorderly conduct.' 1836.
SEAMAN William, s. Samuel and Sarah.
SEAMAN Joseph Henry, s. Samuel and Sarah.
SEAMAN Daniel Holdrick, s. Samuel and Sarah.
SELFE Isaac, chemist and druggist.
    m. Mary Tanner at Sidcot 1798
SERJEANT John of W-s-M, not a member.
    Burial note brought for him 1836
SERJEANT Elizabeth of W-s-M, on list of membs. 1830. d. 1842
SERJEANT John Hill, s. Elizabeth and John.
    Disowned for marrying out 1831.
SERJEANT Robert, s. Elizabeth and John, on list of membs. 1830.
    m. out 13/10/1846. Disowned although they promised to attend mtg. sometimes.
SERJEANT Elizabeth, d. Elizabeth and John.
    m. Martin Lidbetter of SS., at Sidcot 22-11-1843.
SERJEANT Samuel, s. Elizabeth and John.
    m. by priest 1843, and disowned.
SERJEANT Albert Heberdon, not a member.
    Burial note brought for him 1846
§ SESSIONS Wilfred, listed 1887, left by 1888
SHAKLETON Ellis and Fanny
    d. Fanny Elizabeth b. 30/10/1857 reg. in Axbridge.
§ SHARP John, Sidcot rep. 1865, a conchologist.
    Clerk to Sidcot P.M. 1869-69, when he moved away.
§ SHARP Ethel M., listed 1915.
SHARPLES Isaac rec. from John Jenkins' legacy 1728
    Travels 1729,
    m. Hester Thurston of Thornbury, moved to Frenchay MM.
§ SHIELD Sarah, adm. to membs. 1872, having been a pupil and a pupil teacher in SS.

SHIPWAY Ruth, Craigside, Wins.. 1919.
SHOLL E. Margaret, Sandford View, Wins.. Listed 1906
    Moved to Miss Dibble, Trelawney House, Axbridge.
SIMPSON George d. 1863
SMITH Thomas of Cheddar, yeoman, Fit. 1668, d.1692
SMITH Ann of Cheddar, d. of Thomas
    m. James Plumley of Priddy 1681
SMITH John of Axbridge, app. for memb. 1776
SMITH George of Axbridge, shopkeeper.
    Admitted into membership 1820
    m. Mary Strode at Sidcot 1-5-1821, d. 1846
SMITH Letitia, d. George and Mary, resigned 1847
SMITH Mary jnr., d. George and Mary, resigned 1847
SMITH George jnr., s. George and Mary
    Attended another place of worship, resignation accepted 1845
SMITH Strode, s. George and Mary
    On list of membs. 1830, resigned 1847
SMITH John, s. George and Mary, on list of membs. 1830
    d. in infancy.
SMITH John Charles, s. George and Mary
    On list of membs. 1830, d. before 1846.
SMITH Henry Barron, a minister of W-s-M Mtg. and a reg. visitor to Sidcot.
    Ran a school in Weston
    m. § Eliza Ferris of Sidcot 2/7/56
§ SMITH Martha Ecroyd, appointed 1857.
SMITH Till Adam, schoolmaster in W-s-M,
    m. Martha Ann Kingston of W-s-M. 1858.
§ SMITH Cyril F. Spencer, The Cottage, Sidcot. Listed 1908.
    Ethel May
    ch. Mary Lightfoot Spencer.
        John Lightfoot Spencer.
SOMERTON Rachel, poor 1784
§ SPARKES Hannah, listed 1896
SPECIALL William, moved into area 1828.
SPENDER Robert of Winscombe, Banwell and Westbury-sub-Mendip
    put up Richard Plumly but threatened wth indictment 1721
    reg. at MM., often at his house
    Disowned 1746 for "disorderly conduct" with servant.
STEELE Ethel E., Coombe House, Sidcot. Listed 1910.
§ STEPHENS Joseph and son, school gardener in 1847. Was frequent speaker
    in the M.H., and considered a good influence on pupils.
STILE Richard of Burrington, poor, d.1668
STONE Henry of Banwell
    lived with maidservant, disorderly m. at Sidcot 1695. d.1719
    Wife Elizabeth rec. charity money after his death.
STONE Grace of Glastonbury
    m. Abraham Thomas of Winthill 1697
STOUDLY Elizabeth of Axbridge, widow
    m. John Clare 1699
STOUDLY Richard of Axbridge   d.1704
STRANGER William, provided for when ill, 1750
    (prob. from Chew)

QUAKERS AT SIDCOT

STRODE Charles of Allerton applies for memb. 1. 1790 2. 1791
    accepted 1791 (2nd mo.)
    m. Martha Vowles 6th mo. 1791
STRODE Mary d. Chas. and Martha, to Ackworth 1803
    m. George Smith of Axbridge, 1-5-1821.
STRODE Martha d. Chas. and Martha
    To be sent to girl's school at Wellington 1807, d. 30/1/1873
STRODE Hannah d. Chas. and Martha, at SS. 1808
    moved to Bristol 1811
STRODE Rachel d. Chas. and Martha, at SS. 1808, b.1798
    Spent some time in N. America. retnd. 1824.
STRODE Ann d. Chas. and Martha
    resided with Edward Bishop Willmott in Exeter 1809

STRODE Elizabeth d. Chas. and Martha, at SS. 1810
    Went to Philadelphia 1820 with sister Rachel, retnd. 1824.
STRODE Charles s. Chas. and Martha, at SS. 1810
STRODE Sarah d. Chas. and Martha, at SS. 1813, aged 12
    m. out 1828 (Sarah Say), disowned.
STRODE Rebecca d. Chas. and Martha, at SS. 1817.
    m. out 1830 (Rebecca Pitman), disowned.
    Reinstated 1833, having attended mtgs. reg. since her marriage.
STRODE Joseph s. Chas. and Martha, at SS. 1818.
    Moved to Bristol 1820.
STRODE George s. Chas. and Martha
    Killed at SS. about 1820
STRONG Samuel Herbert of Winscombe, listed 1876
STURDGES John of Downend and Langford
    m. Sarah, John Lovell's servant
STURGES Mary d. of John and Sarah
    m. Gabriel Davis Jnr. 1713
STURGES John Jnr. s. of John and Sarah
    defrauds king 1717
    m.1 Rachel Cox of Flax Bourton 1720
    m.2 by priest
STURGE Mary of Bristol, asked permission to use Sidcot MH. for her marriage to
    Wm. A. Tanner. They were m. at Sidcot 23/6/1900.
SYMS Sarah of Banwell, convinced 1770
    m. Joseph Gillet of Somerton, shopkeeper, at Sidcot 3-10-1787

§ TALLACK William, apprenticed in 1845-1852
    Author, and founder of the Howard Ass.,1866.
§ TANGYE Richard, apprentice (released 1852), became engineer,
    formed a firm with his brother George.
TANNER William of Thornbury, Glos., Bleadon and Woodborough
    m.1 Rachel Thomas of Winthill 1740
    m.2 Hannah Vowles of Portishead 1775
    reg. at MM.
TANNER William Jnr. s. Rach. and Wm.
    1st att. MM. 1762
    m. Hannah Curtis 29-3-1771

TANNER William s. Hannah and Wm. ?
  m. Lydia Gregory 4-5-1803
TANNER Thomas of Banwell, s. Mary of Chedzoy, convinced 1770
  m. Sarah Curtis of Banwell 8-5-1770
  reg. at MM., rec. charity money sev. times, Sidcot overseer.
TANNER Mary d. Rach. and Wm.
  m. Edward Harwood of Bristol at Sidcot 21-10-1770
TANNER John s. Rach. and Wm.
  m. Hannah Player of Nailsea 1774, moved to Portishead
TANNER Thomas of Shiplet, Bleadon, Winscombe (and Yarbury?)
  s. Rach. and Wm.
  m. Sarah Bishop of Pensford at Belluton 23-6-1779
TANNER Mary of Winthill, d. Sarah and Thos.
  went to Ackworth 1783, moved to West Div. 1812
TANNER Lydia of Winthill, d. Sarah and Thos..
  m. John Fear of Loxton at Sidcot 1800
TANNER Robert of Winthill s. Sarah and Thos..
  m. Ann Willmott of Yatton, 12-4-1815.
TANNER Mary d. Hannah and Wm.
  m. Isaac Selfe at Sidcot 1798
TANNER Rachel d. Hannah and Wm.
  m. Wm. Allbright Jnr.,shopkeeper, at Sidcot, 1801
TANNER John (of Banwell?) s. Thomas of Yarbury
  m. against rules, disowned 1805
TANNER Abraham of Winthill, grazier, s. Sarah and Thos,
  trustee of Axbridge bur. grd. 1813
  m. Mercy Grace of St. Georges at Portishead 25-7-1816
  app. elder 1860.
TANNER Thomas (Tom) of Winthill, d. 15/9/69 aged 52, of lock-jaw after an
  accident outside the M.H..
TANNER Arthur Thomas s. Hannah and Wm., grazier
  m Mary Gregory of Yatton at Claverham 8-6-1814
  1st reps. Sidcot at MM. 1803
  Clerk of MM. 1818-   d. 16/9/1858
TANNER Mary as above. Reg. minister and traveller.
TANNER William s. A.T. and Mary
  App. minister 1839
  First held public mtgs. 1840. Held many more, often with his mother.
  m. Sarah Wheeler, d. Daniel and Jane Wheeler 13/6/1849 d.11/3/1867
  moved to Bristol, but was a regular visitor.   d. 1866
TANNER Samuel s. A.T. and Mary
  On list of membs. 1830, moved by 1846.
TANNER Arthur s. A.T. and Mary, lived at Oakridge.
  On list of membs. 1830. d. 1869
  m. Margaret Wheeler (born Priestman) 20/4/1855
TANNER Margaret, as above. Outlived husband about 35 years.
TANNER Mary Anna d. A.T. and Mary. On list of membs. 1830.
TANNER James and Mary Gertrude on list of membs. 1870
TANNER Gertrude and James jnr. adm. to membs. 1867
  other ch. Mary Naish b. at Cheddar 24/8/1867
    Gertrude Amy b. at Cheddar 10/7/1871
      John
      Margaret

TANNER William A., from Bristol, asked permission to be m. in Sidcot MH.
　　to Mary Sturge, also of Bristol. They were m. at Sidcot 23/6/1900.
　　Lived in Rose Cottage for a while from 1903.
TANNER [William Edward], Fordlynch, Wins.. Listed 1906.
　　Mary Tregelles
TAYLOR Alfred K. a. 1st listed 1900
THEOBALD Joseph, Clerk to Sidcot P.M. 1860-61.
　　To take care of the chest which contd. the deeds etc..1873
THETCHER Mary of Burrington d. John and Mary
　　m. Thomas Norris of Banwell at Claverham 1723
THETCHER Samuel of Burrington
　　m. Rachel Wreach of Banwell at Claverham 1729
THIELD Sarah, contributed to collections 1873.
§ THISTLETHWAITE William, listed 1886
THOMAS Arthur of Flax Bourton, Barrow Gurney, and Cleeve, yeoman
　　m. Lydia Gundry of Street 1669
　　　reg. at MM., sev. times at his house
THOMAS Abraham of Winthill, Banwell, s. Arthur and Lydia
　　b.1671　d.1732
　　m. Grace Stone 1697
　　reg. at MM.
THOMAS Alice of Axbridge
THOMAS Samuel of Axbridge
THOMAS John of Axbridge　d. very poor 1701
THOMAS John of Winthill s. Abram. and Grace, yeoman b.1714? d.1802
　　overseer of Sidcot Mtg., MM. cashier, clerk of MM.
　　m. Sarah Perris of Long Sutton 1738
THOMAS Grace of Banwell d. Abram. and Grace
　　m. James Fell of Glastonbury, schoolmaster, 1731
THOMAS Rachel of Banwell d. Abram. and Grace
　　m. William Tanner of Kington, Thornbury 1740
THOMAS Grace, overseer of Sidcot Mtg. 1788
THOMPSON Mary Gower　　Listed 1885
　　　Hannah Margaret
　　　　Francis Gower, of Coombe Farm, Sidcot, and Cape Town (1897).
　　Mary Gower moved to Rose Cottage in 1893, others moved away,
THOMPSON [Henry Woolcott] a., of Coombe House, Sidcot. Listed 1905
　　Mary Gower, see above.
§ THOMPSON Sidney, listed 1886
§ THOMPSON John T., Sidcot Schoolmaster from 1901-31.
　　Lived in Rose Cottage, Sidcot.
　　m. Janet F.
　　　ch. John Edmund
　　　　Isabel Valentine
THOMPSON Amy Catherine, Harbury Batch, Sidcot. Listed 1906.
§ THOMPSON Helen G., listed 1918.
THOMPSON Harold S., Bristol, listed 1919.
§ THORNTON Philip L. adm. to membs. 1850 d. soon after.
§ THORP Alice, on Comm. for Summer School 1905.

TREGELLES Hannah Margaret, Cardiff, nrm. 1893
    (wife of Thomas S. T.)
    ch. David
        Gower
    Moved to Coombe House, Sidcot (1921 list)
TRIPP Lily a. 1st listed 1890. m. and moved to B'gham about 1893.
TRIPP Edward a. 1st listed 1890.
TUCKER Hannah of Butcombe
    m. Richard Hipsley 1696
TUGWELL Mary of Winscombe
    m. Gabriel Ballot of Wedmore 1691
TULLY George with wife and son moved to Charterhouse 1789
    son Francis apprenticed in Bristol 1801
    moved to Bristol bankrupt in 1805 but not to blame
TURNBULL Gertrude, listed 1907.

§ VEALE John Edey and Hannah, filled in as Superintendents in 1846.
VOWLES Thomas of Nempnett memb. of Chew mtg.
    m. Mary Curtis (widow) 1755
VOWLES Martha d. Joseph Vowles of Wrington
    m. Charles Strode 1791
VOWLES Hannah of Portishead
    m. Wm. Tanner of Woodborough (widdower)
VOWLES Joseph of Wrington and Stone Allerton, taylor.
    at MM. 1794
VOWLES Abel, neglected attendance at mtg.
    m. by priest 1798

WADDINGTON Rachel, on list of membs. 1830, moved by 1846.
§ WALKER Frances M.,listed 1885.
WALLER Fanny Martin, on list of membs. 1830, moved by 1846.
§ WALLER Nancy, listed 1908.
WALTER Peter of Hollatrow, Fit 1668,   d.1700
    m.1. Suzanna Clement of Hallatrow 1663, d.1671
    m.2. Mary Plummer of Burrington 1673
    reg. at MM.
§ WARDELL Annie, contributed to collections 1872.
§ WATSON Jane, listed 1875.
WATSON George Alston, listed 1918.
    Esther
    ch. Alison Mary.
WATTS William of Nempnett, poor
    m. Rebekah
    admonished by Gen. Mtg. 1668
    rec. from Wm. Reeve's legacy, and John Jenkins legacy.
    Advised to move nearer a mtg. 1712
WATTS John bro. of Wm. also advised by Friends 1712
WATTS Mary d. of Wm. of Nempnett
    m. Wm. Stringer 1715
WEARE James
    had a crippled daughter.
    received from John Chappell's legacy 1712

QUAKERS AT SIDCOT

WEARE Millicent, poor
   conduct not acceptable, so Frds. not easy to give her money, 1714.
WEDMORE Richard, poor man, "feeble" 1705.
WELSH Peter of Sidcot, adm. into membs. 1816.
WELSH Harriet of Sidcot app. for membs. and accepted 1821.
   ch. Peter and Edward also accepted 1822.
WEST Edward, The Glen, Wins. listed 1915.
   m. Louisa
   ch. Edward Gundry.
WEST Edward Gundry, Keatly P.O., Saskatchewan, Canada. Listed 1915.
WESTWOOD James a. listed 1901
WHALLEY Thomas. S.Schoolmaster 1813-1820
   wife Rachel and ch. Sophia, Eliza, and Thomas Patchet,
   moved to Canada 1820.
§ WHARTON Florence A., moved to Liverpool, 1902.
WHEELER Ann, on list of membs. 1830.
WHITE Ann of Stour Provost Dorset
   m. Thomas Reeve of Woodborough 1699
WHITE James of Hutton
   m. Joanna Davis of Banwell at Sidcot 1742
WHITE Susannah d. James and Joanna
   m. by priest 1762
WHITE Phoebe d. James and Joanna
   had a bastard child and disowned 1774
WHITEHEAD John of Bruton, Clothier,   b,1669 d.1714
   Sarah Lawrence 1696
WHITING John of Nailsea, Longsutton, Wrington and London,
   yeoman, then linen draper. b.1656 d.1722
   In Wrington from 1688-1699 after 8yrs in prison.
   m. Sarah Hurd 1686
WHITLOW Charles Henry, listed 1896
   c/o Richard Binns, Coombehurst, Sidcot.
WILLIAMS Edwin Arthur, Sidcot rep. 1864.
   Moved away 1861.
§ WILLIAMS Anna Maria, listed 1875
§ WILLIAMS Katie, MM.rep. 1903.
§ WILLIAMS Katherine, listed 1918.
WILLIS Timothy of Rowberrow, yeoman. Fit 1668   d.1698
   m.1. Joan   d.1688
   m.2. Sarah Davis at Cheddar 1690   d.1699
WILLIS Mary of Rowberrow, d. Thomas, neice Timothy
   m. Wm. Reeve 1687
§ WILLIS Janet, listed 1879
§ WILLIS Dorothy, listed 1910.
WILLMOTT Robert at Sidcot for a short time 1792-
   before moving to Chew
WILLMOTT Joseph at MM. 1795
   m. contrary to rules and disowned 1802, reinstated 1813
WILLMOTT Robert of Pensford, shopkeeper, s. Edward and Mary of Bristol
   m. Sarah Benwell at Sidcot 9-11-1804
   Clerk of MM.
WILLMOTT Martha, Sidcot Overseer 1813

WILLMOTT Frederick, South Hill, Sandford, listed 1916
WILSON Agnes of Weymouth
    m. Wm. Lawrence 1691
§ WILSON Mary, on staff during Bevan Lean's time, app. for membs. about 1915
WILSON Jean C. a., listed 1920.
WOOD Francis a Sidcot rep..14/3/1860
    P.M. Clerk during 1860.
§ WOOD Eva Gertrude, MM. rep. 7th mo. 1900, left 1905.
WOOD Francis William, Clerk to Sidcot P.M. 1859-60.
WOOD Margt. Page? a., listed 1918.
WOOKEY Rose a., listed 1908.
§ WORSDELL Margaret, listed 1918.
WREACH James of Congresbury
    m. Mary Hipsley of Churchill 1721
WREACH Rachel of Banwell
    m. Samuel Thetcher of Burrington 1729
WREACH Lydia "belongs to Sidcott meeting"
    m. by priest and behaved in "scandalous manner" 1750

YATES Margaret a., listed 1907.
YEALES Ann, d.Mary Hipsley of Churchill
    m. Gabriel Davis 1677
YEEPE Richard of Cheddar, "a very poor man", Fit 1668   d.1693
YEEPE Richard Jnr. of Cheddar
    "kept company" before m. by priest
    rec. charity 1734, moved into Claverham MH. 1834
YOUNG Mary
YOUNG George (or John) of Priddy, labourer
    goods taken 1670

LIST OF MEMBERS AND ATTENDERS OF SIDCOT MEETING FIRST LISTED FROM 1922

* attender; a associate member; + member of another meeting
(m ...) married to ... [non-attending spouse]
(w ...) widow or widower of ...
The year following each name is that when it first appears on the printed list.

+ ABBATT, C PAUL.   1923
  ABSALOM, FRANCES.   1964
+ ABSALOM, JOHN.   1964
  ALEXANDER, NORMAN JACK.
       Vancouver Island BC 1980
  ALLEN, ALYSON.   1983
  ALLEN, BARRY.   1983
       Charlotte
       Edward Joseph Frank
       Dickon Frederick Arthur
+ ALLEN, PHYLLIS STAFFORD.   1929
  ALLETSON, JANET LILIAN.   1966
  ALLETSON, PETER GEORGE.   1966
       Philip John
       Susan Elizabeth
  ALLETSON, SUSAN ELIZABETH. (m David Champion)   Alberta 1983
  ANDREWS, ERICA. (m David)   1978
* APPLEBY, A WINIFRED.   1954
* ARMFIELD, LEONARD.   1928
       * Audrey
       * Stuart M
* ARMFIELD, MALCOLM.   1951
  ARMITAGE, FRANCIS W.   1938
* ARMITAGE, IRENE L.   1938
       * John Wallis
       * Judith Keren
       Roger Thomas
  ARMITAGE, MARY G.   1949
  ARNOLD, JANET MARY.   1968
  ARNOLD, JOHN.   1968
       * Hilary
       * Peter
       * Nancy
  ASHBY, ALICE.   1937
  ATTOE, BARBARA.   1983
  ATTOE, PETER.   1983
       * Rebecca Mary
       * Kathryn Jane

  BAILEY, ELIZABETH M.   1985
  BAILEY, TIMOTHY A.   1985
       * Thomas
       * Alice
       * Oliver
  BAKER, JULIET E.   1966
  BAKER, WILSON.   1966
  BAKER, KAY.   1976
  BAKER, KENNETH E.   1976
+ BAKER, ROSALIND MARY.   1970
* BAKER, WINIFRED. (m Tom)   1976
  BAMFORD, SUSAN. (m Anthony)   1987
       * Bryony
       * Amelia
  BANNER, ALICE E.   1949
  BANNER, BERNARD.   1949
       Mary E
* BARKLA, CHARLES JOLLY.   1930
* BARKLA, EMMA JANE.   1930
  BARNES, HAZEL MARGARET.   1943
* BARNES, WILLIAM.   1943
+ BARRETT, EDITH.   1945
  BARRINGTON, NICHOLAS.   1971
* BARRINGTON, ROLANDE.   1971
       * Piers
       * Miles
  BASTIN, HELEN M.   1925
  BATTEN, CHRISTOPHER R.   1967
  BATTEN, MARGARET W.   1969
       Linda Margaret
       Philip Michael
       Jennifer Karen
  BEER, TERENCE. (m Kathleen)   1969
  BEN-TOVIM, JOSEPHINE MARY. (m David)   1978
       * Kate
  BERG, JONATHAN.   1983
  BERG, MARY. (m Jan H)   1974
       + David A
       + Stella A
       Jonathan
* BERRY, MARK.   1957
* BERRY, ROWENA.   1957
       * David
       * Christopher
       * Patrick

147

QUAKERS AT SIDCOT

BIRKBECK, HENRY J. 1971
BIRKBECK, MARGARET. 1971
* BLACKMAN, JOANNA. (m Alan) 1985
  * Sadie
  * Rhiannon
  * Emma
BLANDFORD, JOHN WILLIAM. 1975
* BOARD, TREVOR. 1953
+ BOBBETT, CHRISTOPHER. (m Florence Ruby D) 1945
BOBBETT, FLORENCE ADA. 1943
BOBBETT, MARGARET E. 1945
BOBBETT, SYDNEY FOX. (m Marjorie H 1950) 1945
* BODYCOTE, EMMA. 1968
+ BODYCOTE, JOHN H. 1968
BOOBYER, CRISTINE. 1960
* BOOBYER, DESMOND G. 1960
  Ian Charles
  Jacqueline Diana
  Sally
* BOOBYER, DOROTHY. 1943
BOOBYER, GEORGE H. 1943
  * Desmond G
  * Jennifer M
BOOKER, WINIFRED K. 1989
BOURGOIN, EDVIGE FRANCE. 1923
* BOWYER, PETER. 1989
BRADLEY, F HELEN. 1954
BRADLEY, JAMES T. 1954
  Anne E
  Jennifer
  Susan
  Andrew John
BRADY, EDITH M. 1952
BRADY, WILLIAM. 1928
  Edith
BRAYSHAW, KATHLEEN A. 1958
BRAYSHAW, RICHARD N. 1958
  Deborah A K
BROOKE, EMILY. 1966
BROOKE, WILLIS. 1966
BROOKES, ISABEL. 1979
BROWN, DOROTHY. (m William) 1960
BROWN, JEREMY. 1978
BROWN, JOHN E. 1981
BROWN, MARGARET H. 1981
* BROWN, JUDI. 1987
BROWN, PETER W. (m Alison) 1978
  * Tessa Joanne
  * Michael Andrew

BROWN, VIOLET MAUD. 1957
BROWN, WILLIAM. 1957
  Daphne M
  Valerie J
  Peter W
BRUCE, MARGARET BLANCHE. (m William) 1942
  Michael
BUCKLAND, DENIS S. 1951
* BUGLAS, EFFIE. 1943
* BUGLAS, HILAIRE. 1943
+ BULLARD, DAVID. 1976
+ BUNNEY, STEPHEN. 1983
BUNYARD, FRANCES BARBARA. 1947
BURCHAM, EMMA KATE. 1930
BURCHAM, MARGARET EMILY. 1930
BURGE, JANE. (m Brian) 1973
  * Mark
  * Tony
  * Sarah
  * David
* BURROWS, DOROTHY. 1980
* CAMERON, CONSTANCE. 1931

CANNON, . 1971
  * Jonathan
  * Peter
CARLILE, RUPERT. 1983
* CARTER, SUZANNE. 1971
  CASHMORE, ANTHONY R. 1970
* CASHMORE, ROSALIND M. 1970
  Corinne
  Lindsay
CASHMORE, LINDSAY. 1978
* CHADWICK, FLORENCE E. 1971
* CHADWICK, MARION. 1931
CHAMP, MARTHA L. San Francisco 1928
* CHAPMAN, B BURGOYNE. 1929
* CHAPMAN, ELIZABETH GOUCHER. 1929
* CHILTON, JENNIFER MARY. 1964
CLARK, HELEN SOPHIA HEATH. (m Roderick K) 1942
  Edmund Kendall
  John Horne
+ CLARK, JOHN. 1940
+ CLARK, JOYCE EVELYN. 1940
  Ann
  Janet
CLARK, JOSEPHINE. 1928
CLOTHIER, EUSTACE HENRY. 1923

QUAKERS AT SIDCOT

CLOTHIER, RHODA ESTHER. 1923
   Hilda
COATS, JEAN MARGARET. (m Ronald
   Leonard) 1964
   [Paul Newton]
COLLINGS, BERTHA I.W.. 1927
* COLLINS, SUSAN. 1987
COLLINSON, HUGH. 1971
COLLINSON, MURIEL. 1971
* CONNAH, SARAH H. 1931
* COOK, PETER. 1931
* COOPER, MARY. 1954
COOPER, MAY. 1927
* COOPER, STELLA. 1937
COPE, VERA. 1964
   Pamela Guida
COTTAM, JOAN MARGARET. 1960
COTTAM, RICHARD. 1960
   Sheila Elaine
+ COTTERELL, A P I. 1937
   + Annie M
+ COTTERELL, ARTHUR N. 1928
COUSINS, ANNIE L. 1964
+ COVENTRY, HILDA MARGARET. 1928
COYSH, R HENRY. 1976
COYSH, LILIAN E. 1976
CRAPPER, EDITH B. 1943
+ CROSFIELD, ANNA C. 1945
+ CROSS, DAVID G. (m Judith) 1976
   * Huw David
   * Gareth Thomas
CROSSLEY, HILDA. 1929
CUMBER, MIRA LOUISA. Sz-chwan
   Province, China 1925
CURTIS, DAVID. 1989
CUSHNIE, JOSEPHINE MARY. 1970
CUSHNIE, WILLIAM BARNABAS. 1950
CUSHNIE, DORIS LOUISE. 1950
   Valerie Louise
   Josephine Mary
* CUSHNIE, GWENLLIAN. 1970

DANN, FREDA SOUTHALL. St Ives 1947
+ DARBYSHIRE, MARY. 1938
+ DARBYSHIRE, PHILLIP H. 1938
   + Brian
DARE, GERTRUDE ADELE. 1942
DARE, JOSEPH H S. 1942
* DAVIES, DOREEN. 1943
DAVIES, THOMAS BARRY. 1943
DAVIES, LESLIE ELEANOR. (m George
   M L) 1933
   * Jane H

DE SAULLE, FRANCES MARY. 1940
DE SAULLE, FREDERICK H. 1940
DELANEY, ANNIE. 1971
DICKINSON, DONALD. 1923
DICKINSON, HENRY B. 1940
* DICKINSON, MAUD. 1940
   Margaret Edna
DICKMAN, ANN L. (m Anthony) 1985
+ DILKS, ARTHUR BRUCE. 1928
   DIXON, IAIN. (m Margaret) 1966
   Martin Iain
   Phillipa
DIXON, KATHLEEN. 1938
DIXON, RALPH. 1938
   * Margaret
   * Ian
DIXON, SARAH. 1938
DODINGTON, MARTHA L. 1925
   Sven Henry Marriott
   Robin Björn Marriott
DODINGTON, ROBIN B M. 1935
DODINGTON, SVEN HENRY M. 1929
DODINGTON, ROBIN B M. 1929
DONCASTER, DORA PRIESTMAN.
   1923
   Gertrude Marian
   Doris Winifred
   Leonard Hugh
* DORAN, MARGARET C. 1929
DORAN, WILLIAM. 1929
   Eithné Marguerite
   Archibald Lester
   David Moore
* DOUGLAS, ANNE M. 1971
+ DOUGLAS, GEORGE B. 1971
   * David A
   * Paul
   * John Christopher
* DOUGLAS, GEORGE. 1964
DOWMAN, MARGARET. 1950
DRAKEFORD, IMOGEN. 1976
DRAKEFORD, ROBERT. 1976
   * Andrew
   * Philippa
   * David
* DUNIAM-JONES, DOROTHY. 1954
* DeVOTE, JANE. (m Derek) 1978
   * Milou

EDBROOKE, EDYTH. 1972
ELLIOTT, JANET MARY. 1931
ELLIOTT, THOMAS CHARLES. 1931
   John Huxtable

ELLIS, JANE. (m Ian M)   1974
+ ENGEL, ELIZABETH.   1975
ENGLISH, MARGARET B. (m Brian
   Arthur John   1952
   Marcus
+ ENNOR, MONICA. (m Douglas Wilfred)
   1952
ETTLINGER, DAPHNE H C.   Toronto
   1966
FAIRCLOUGH, MABEL.   Vancouver Is
   land, BC   1926
FARRELL, ETHEL MAY.   1957
FARRELL, JAMES WILLIAM.   1957
FAWELL, RUTH. (m G Scott)   1964
FELCE, JOSEPH.   1956
FELCE, NAN D.   1956
   David
   Josephine A
   Christine E
FELCE, JOSEPHINE.   1958
FENTON, ANNIE.   1942
FENTON, WALTER.   1942
FENTON, CYRIL RAWLETT.   1942
FENTON, GLENYS.   1942
   Philip Rawlett
   Patricia Anne
+ FINCH, OLIVE P.   1937
+ FITTON, EDITH.   1942
+ FITTON, LAURENCE R.   1942
   Eleanor Joy
FLETCHER, BASIL A.   1955
FOGGO, MARGARET EDNA. (m Arthur)
   1964
FRANCIS, BERYL M.   1983
FRANCIS, H BASIL.   1983
* FRANKS, KATHARINE SHEWELL.
   1940
* FRANKS, ROBERT R.   1940
* FRANKS, MARY.   1942
* FRANKS, RICHARD.   1942
FREEM, GRACE MURIEL.
FREEM, JOHN A.   1957
* FREEM, MINNIE OLIVE.   1957
   Grace Muriel

GAGE, ELEANOR.   1967
   Nigel F
* GASTER, DAVID.   1987
GAY, KATHARINE.   1974
* GAY, TIMOTHY.   1974
   * Mark Wilson
   * Nicholas

   * Benjamin
GAYNER, CHARLOTTE.   1928
   Elsie C
   Helen Lucy
* GERRETT, STELLA. (m Henry)   1980
GERTNER, ZOE.   1980
GIBBINS, CECIL.   1931
GIBBINS, EMILY MARY.   1931
   Francis Bevington
   Norman Henry
   Hellen Tregelles
GIBBINS, NORMAN H.   Atbara, Sudan
   1937
* GIBSON, CONSTANCE ELAINE.   1933
* GIBSON, STANTON.   1933
   * Helen
   * Francis Edward Thomas
GIBSON, JOCELYNN.   1967
GOODING, KATHLEEN M.   1985
GOSTICK, CONSTANCE M.   1925
GRAY, BETTY COLQUHOUN.   1945
GRAY, C IVAN.   1945
   Robin
   Andrea Judith
* GREAVES, KENNETH C.   1952
GREAVES, ROBIN VIPONT MARY.
   1952
   Richard Stephen
   Deborah Mary
   Caroline
GREEN, IRENE.   1947
GREENFIELD, CHRISTOPHER.   1987
GREENFIELD, GILLIAN.   1987
   * Alexander George
+ GREGORY, ELIZA. (m THOMAS C)
   1937
+ GREGORY, JOAN M.   1947
GREGORY, MARJORIE J.   1949
GREGORY, MURIEL E.   Clapham, Lon
   don. 1931
* GREY, MURIEL.   1925
* GRIFFIN, A SERCOMBE.   1923
GRIFFIN, DOROTHY.   1923
   * Alfred George Kenneth
   * Margaret Blanche
* GRIFFIN, ALFRED GEORGE KEN
   NETH.   1942
* GRIFFIN, MARGARET.   1942
GRIFFIN, FRANCES E. (m WILLIAM H)
   1949
GRIMSHAW, WINIFRED MARY.   1946

GRUBB, DAVID.   1925
   * Elizabeth A
   * John B
   * Gawen K
GRUBB, EDWARD DIXON.   1937
* GRUBB, KATHLEEN.   1937
GRUBB, ELIZABETH.   1923
GUNDRY, VALERIE A. (m Christopher) 1973
   * Sarah Louise
   * Helen Rachel

HADDEN, HELEN MARGARET.   1936
* HADDON, MARGARET. (m John)   1954
   * John Richard
   [Sally Miranda]
HALLIDAY, M ANNE.   1950
HARMAN, GILLIAN M.   1949
HARMAN, R ALEC.   1949
* HARMAN, IDA.   1925
* HARMAN, RICHARD A.   1925
   * Michael Alexander
   Ida Alanur
* HARRIS, CHRISTINA.   1978
HARRIS, DESMOND.   1978
   * Shannon
   * Katie
   * Benjamin
HARRISSON, ROGER G R.   1940
HAVARD, SHEILA ELAINE.   Montreal 1974
HAWKES, CHRISTOPHER.   1974
HAWKES, ELIZABETH.   1974
   Sarah Jane
   Jeremy John
   Nicholas
HAWKES, MARGARET. (w Reginald) 1983
HAYGARTH, MARGARET.   1929
HEALEY, ELIZABETH. (m John)   1975
HEANEY, E JOAN.   1971
HEATH, DAISY.   1971
HEATH, EDITH.   1971
HEATH, FLORENCE.   1923
HEDGER, LILIAN JOSEPHINE.   1928
* HEDGER, RALPH WESTAWAY.   1928
* HEMMINGS, MARGARET.   1976
HEWITT, JOAN.   1975
* HEWLETT, HUGH.   1987
HIGGINS, DULCIE EVELINE.   1951

* HIGGINS, JOHN F.   1956
   Miller, Adrian Blake
   Miller, Deidre Carol
HILL, AUBREY F.   1983
HILL, GILLIAN M.   1983
   * Alison Ruth
   * Marian Jane
HINTON, E RICHARD.   1966
HINTON, JOYCE.   1966
   * Jacqueline Anne
   * Jonathan Nigel
   * Angela Mary
HITCHINGS, BESSIE.   1928
HITCHINGS, THOMAS MAURICE.   1928
HOLLAND, MALCOLM E.   1975
+ HOOPER, E MARY.   1945
HOPES, I AUBREY.   1949
HOPES, ANN.   1949
   Gareth
   Jeffrey
HOPES, GRACE.   1978
HORNE, MURIEL S.   1952
HORNE, PERCY.   1942
HOUGHTON, BEATRICE. (w Harold) 1971
   Nevil H
   Carol L
   J Russell
HUGHES, EMILY.   Harbury Batch   1960
HUGHES, HERBERT.   1983
HUGHES, RENATA.   1983
HUMPHRIES, IONA.   1966
HUSSEY, DEREK.   1970
HUSSEY, GRACE.   1970
   Jane
HUTCHINSON, CHRISTOPHER WEST.   1925
HUTCHINSON, GEORGE WOODS.   1925
I'ANSON, EDWARD JOHN. (m Kathleen Helen)   1966

ILIFF, NAOMI. (m Mark)   Birmingham 1976
IRONSIDE, DONALD JAMES.   1972
IRONSIDE, JEAN.   1972

* JAMES, ERIC.   1968

151

QUAKERS AT SIDCOT

* JAMES, MYRTLE.   1968
   * Thomas Webley
   * Stephen Eric
   * Gwyneth Margaret
   * Meryn Winn
   * Owen Robert
+ JAMES, FIONA SIOBHAN. (m Stephen T) 1985
   * Rebecca (Powell)
   * Eleanor (Powell)
   * Jacob (Powell)
JEFFERIES, FREDERICK CHARLES BOULTON.   1925
JEFFERIES, LILY.   1925
   Douglas
   Richard Douglas
JEFFERIES, RICHARD DOUGLAS.   1942
JEFFREE, CHRISTOPHER E. (m Julia) 1983
   * Megan Rachel
JEFFREE, DAPHNE.   1976
JEFFREE, EDWARD.   1976
   Christopher
   Martin
   Anthony
JEFFREE, MARTIN A. (m Carol)   1978
   * Rebecca A
   * Timothy Edward
JEREMIAH, KEITH C.   1950
JEREMIAH, MARGARET GORDON.   1950
   Katharine Gordon
   Helen Gordon
   Keith Bernard Christian
* JOHNSON, MARGARET.   1989
* JONES, DOROTHY M.   1966
JONES, FREDERICK A.   1966
* JUPE, MARY JANE.   1926
   JUST, ELFRIDA A E.   1939

* KAY, NESTA. (m Harry)   1978
+ KELSALL, NORA.   1964
+ KERNEY, CLOUD ABIGAIL.   1972
   KIDDER, ANNE MARIE.   1960
* KIDDER, DOUGLAS E.   1960
* KING, MARGARET L.   1970
   KING, THOMAS R.   1970
      Rosemary
+ KINOOVKIS, V SANDRA.   1966
   KIPPAX, RUTH H. (m John)   1949
   KNIGHT, D CHRISTOPHER.   1985
   KNIGHT, HOWARD M.   1976

KNIGHT, JENNIFER.   1976
   * Christopher
   * Elizabeth
   * Rachel

* LAMB, GEORGE ERIC SEVERN.   1923
+ LAMB, WINIFRED.   1923
   * Peter Severn
+ LANSDOWNE, MARY E MABBETT. 1964
LE MERE, MONICA.   1935
LE PETIT, JESSIE.   1932
LEAKER, EMMA BEATRICE.   1939
+ LEAN, KATHERINE DILYS.   1927
LEAN, OWEN B. (m Doreen M)   1929
   Jennifer Elizabeth
   Anthony Bevan
   John Bevan
LEE, BEATRICE LUCY.   1954
* LEE, WILLIAM HURRELL.   1954
LEE, MICHAEL O'C.   1954
LEIMDORFER, THOMAS C.   1978
LEIMDORFER, VALERIE.   1978
   * Andrew
   * Gilliam
   * Karen
LEWIS, E MARY.   1978
LEWIS, HENRY H.   1978
LINDLEY, ALISON JANE. (m Heiner Josenhans) Nova Scotia 1976
LINDLEY, DAVID.   1964
* LINDLEY, JOYCE MURIEL.   1964
   Alison Jane
   Peter James
LINNEY, CECILIA W.   1933
LINNEY, RICHARD KENNETH.   1933
LINNEY, CHARLES KEITH. (m Dorothy) 1938
LINNEY, FRANCIS STEWART.   1925
LINNEY, GEORGE FREDERICK.   1927
LINNEY, GERTRUDE MARY.   1927
   Richard Kenneth
   Kathleen Margaret
   Charles Keith
LITTEN, ALAN FREDERICK.   1974
LITTEN, BRUCE O. (m Norah L)   1946
+ LITTEN, HERBERT OSBORNE.   1932
+ LITTEN, MARGARET WALLACE.   1932
   + Herbert Wallace
   + Lionel Corder
   + Bruce Osborne
   + Hazel Margaret
   + Donald Ivor

LITTEN, HERBERT WALLACE.   1949
LITTEN, OLIVE MARY.   1949
   Jean Margaret
   Alan Frederick
   Malcolm Oliver
   Alison Mary
LITTEN, MALCOLM OLIVER.   1973
* LITTEN, DIANE.   1973
   * Natasha Sarah
   * Jennifer Rachel
LITTLE, AMY.   1943
LITTLE, WALTER.   1943
LITTLEBOY, CHRISTINE M.   1925
LITTLEBOY, GERALD.   1928
LITTLEBOY, GWENDOLINE.   1928
   Eleanor
LITTLEBOY, MAURICE.   1923
LLOYD, MARGARET.   1942
   Elizabeth M
   M Anne
   C Judith
+ LLOYD, W ARNOLD.   Woodbrooke, Selly Oak 1943
LOCKWOOD, SALLY MARY. (m Martin) 1975
* LOGIE, HELEN M.   1925
LONGMAN, FRANCEYS R. (w Arnold) 1974
LOW, K MARJORIE.   1925
LUCAS, OLIVE.   1955
   Daphne H C
LUNN, SUE.   1983
LYALL, FRANCES.   1972

+ MAJOR, KATHARINE. (w John)   1971
MAJOR, VALERIE.   1989
MALCOLM, HILDA. (m Louis W G)   1952
MALLEN, CORINNE. (m Tony)   1974
MANLEY, MAUD. (m George)   1946
MARRIAGE, PERSIS M.   1971
MARRIAGE, ROBERT. (m Hazel)   1925
   [Veronica]
   [Robert]
MARSDEN, ARTHUR.   1981
MARSDEN, ROSALIND.   1981
* MARSDEN, HAZEL.   1988
MARSHALL, H DONNE.   1978
MARSHALL, P JULIA.   1978
   * Helen
   * Peter
* MATTHEWS, JOHN.   1989
* MATTHEWS, SALLY.   1989

MAW, HUGH W.   1945
* MAYBERY, ELLA. (m Frank)   1923
   * Joyce
   * Ruth
   * Nancy
a MAYER, BESSIE.   1925
MERRICK, DEBORAH.   1987
   * Neave
METFORD, MATILDA.   1925
MILLER, ADRIAN BLAKE.   1968
MILLER, DEIDRE CAROL.   1964
* MILLER, DULCIE EVELINE.
   (m Frederick) 1950
   * Adrian Blake
   * Deidrie Carol
+ MILLER, JOHN S.   1940
+ MILLER, NANCY R.   1940
   John Simon
   Teresa Margaret
MILLS, MARY. (m Eric)   1971
   Sally Brown
   Simon Brown
   Cherry Brown
   Jeremy Brown
* MILNER, JAMES HILEY.   St Ives 1940
MILNER, LUCY HELEN.   1940
MITTON, EVA LORRAINE.   1923
MITTON, WILLIAM HENRY.   1923
+ MOGRIDGE, ENA.   1973
MORGAN, ESTHER. (m Donald)   1987
MUDGE, ALISON.   1971
MURRAY, CONSTANCE. (w John)   1981
MURRAY-RUST, DAVID M.   1947
MURRAY-RUST, FRANCES K.   1947
   Peter
   Alan
   D Hammond
MURRELL, K F HYWEL.   1937
MUSSELL, DOROTHY.   1951
MUSSELL, HENRY.   1951
* MYERS, KEVAN.   1983
* MYERS, SUSANNAH.   1988
MacMAHON, ROSEMARY. (m John) 1980
   * Sheena
   * Andrew
MacQUEEN, SANDRA. (m James)   1985
   * Adam
McGNAGH, DEBORAH A K. (m Stanley) 1971

QUAKERS AT SIDCOT

McINTOSH, E MARGARET. (m John Newton) 1933
   John Anthony Carrick
* McLEOD, EILEEN. (m John) 1942
* McMICHAEL, FANNIE. 1923
McMICHAEL, P JANET. (m Anthony John) 1971
   * Lee John Robert
   * Jessica

NASH, . 1971
   * Heather
   * Elizabeth
   * Katrina
NEATBY, HELEN M J. 1931
NICHOL, CHRISTINE. 1987
   * Lorna WILSON
NICHOL, DAVID. 1987
NICHOL, ROSEMARY. 1987
   * Katie
   * Toby
   * Clare
   * Vicky
NORIE, I JOAN. Vancouver Island, BC 1978
NOTT, CHERRY. (m Martin) 1978

OSBORNE, ELIZABETH. 1925

* PACKER, MARGERITA M. 1956
PACKER, PHILIP R. 1956
   * Robert N
   * John R
* PAGE, LUCY. 1925
PAGE, RACHEL. 1951
+ PAGE-WOOD, A GLADYS. 1973
* PALMER, GRACE DOROTHY MAY. 1935
PALMER, WILLIAM NATHANIEL. 1935
   * Henry
   * John
   * Humphrey
PASK, BARBARA MARY. 1966
PASK, EDITH ALICE. 1925
PASK, ROWLAND W. 1925
   Barbara Mary
PASSINGHAM, MURIEL. 1951
+ PAWSON, MARIANNE. (m Mark) 1980
   * Andrew M
PEARCE, FIONA. 1976

* PEARCE, FRANCIS H. 1976
   Alan Christopher
   Simon Martin
PEARCE, GEOFFREY. (m Heather) 1981
   * Andrew
   * Juliet
   * Stephen
   * Philip
* PEARCE, GRACE JANET. 1933
+ PEET, GILBERT EDWARD. (m Margaret Octavia) 1931
   * Margaret Love
   * Alice Edrey Louisa
PEILE, ALICE M. 1953
PERRY-SMITH, HELEN T. 1960
   * Christopher
   * Katherine
PERYER, DAVID. 1971
PERYER, DINAH. 1971
   * Jonathan
   * David
   * Jane
* PETERS, MARGARET. 1945
PETERS, RICHARD S. 1945
* PETERS, WINIFRED. 1950
* PHILIP, FLORENCE PENROSE. 1938
+ PHILLIPS, EVELYN B. 1942
PIKE, AGNES J. 1928
PIKE, STANLEY O. 1928
PITT, ISAAC. Malay States 1925
PLANT, JEAN. 1976
* PLANT, KENNETH. 1976
   * Joanna
   * Tom
* POWELL, DENISE. 1985
PRIEST, FRANCIS E. (m Marie Beatrix) 1969
PROCTER, CHRYSTABEL P G. 1971

RADLEY, PATRICK F. 1964
RADLEY, G CLAIRE. 1964
   Nicholas
   Peter
   Christine
* RASTRICK, MARGARET. 1955
REDFERN, CECILY. 1929
REDFERN, ERICA. 1925
REDFERN, STANLEY. 1925
   Foster
   Cicily
   Peter
REDFERN, FOSTER. 1929

* REDFERN, MARJORIE.   1943
    Julia Mary
    Helen Ruth
  REDFERN, PETER.   1929
+ REED, L GORDON.   1967
* REED, WINIFRED MARY.   1967
    + Robert Philip
    * Alison Jane
  REINGE, E LILIAN.   1966
+ REINGE, ROLAND JOSEPH.   1966
  REINGE, IVY MARGERY.   1950
* REINGE, SIDNEY GEORGE.   1950
    * Shirley
    * Paul Braybrook
  RENDELL, CELIA J. (m Peter)   1952
    [Anthony Fairfax]
    [Annie Leslie]
    [David Michael]
  REYNOLDS, JOAN.   1956
+ RICHARDSON, GWENDOLINE F.   1923
  RICKS, ESMIE.   1983
  RICKS, LAURIE.   1987
  ROBERTS, EVELYN.   1938
  ROBERTS, HELEN LOUISA. (m Samuel) 1925
    Joseph Maurice
  ROBERTS, JOSEPH MAURICE.   1938
  ROBERTS, STANLEY THOMAS HARLAND.   1942
  ROBSON, EDGAR MANN.   1947
  ROBSON, MARIA BROADHEAD.   1947
  ROBSON, HENRY ISAAC.   1939
  ROBSON, HILDA M.   1939
  ROBSON, JOHN S.   1973
  ROBSON, EDITH S.   1973
  ROBSON, S BARBARA.   1964
  ROPER, JACQUELINE. (m Peter)   1987
    * Mark (Tuxill)
    * Catherine
* ROSEVEARE, MARJORY.   1966
  ROSEVEARE, WILLIAM L.   1966
  ROWLANDS, ALBERT.   1935
* ROWLANDS, MARY.   1935
    Thomas Peter
    Mary Howarth
    Albert David
    Catherine Ada
    Paul
+ ROWLANDS, EDITH ANNIE.   1931
  ROWLANDS, PAUL. (m Ruth)   1956
  ROWLING, VALERIE J. (m Mark)   1974

ROWNTREE, MARGARET THERESE.   1943
+ RUSSELL, MARGARET.   1975
+ RUTTER, DOROTHY C.   1927

SADLER, JOHN. (m Evelyn)   1978
SAINSBURY, ANNIE. (m Herbert)   N America   1925
SALISBURY, JEAN M.   1964
SAMPSON, OLIVE C.   1936
SAYCE, EDITH ALICE. (m Douglas Edward)   Bournemouth   1935
    [Hugh Bevan]
    [Rosalind Mary]
    [Jonathan Brian]
* SAYCE, HUGH.   1953
* SAYCE, MOLLIE.   1953
    * Rosemary
    * Roderick
* SCHULTZ, LOUISE M J.   1923
  SCHWARTZ, REBECCA. (w Jack)   1985
a SEAMAN, MOLLIE.   1987
a SEAMAN, RAY.   1987
  SECCOMBE, RICHARD.   1980
+ SEWELL, ARNOLD E.   1951
+ SEWELL, MARGUERITE E.   1951
  SEWELL, LEONIE.   1964
* SEWELL, ROGER C.   1964
    Andrew Peter
  SHAKESPEARE, ISOBEL. (m Thomas)   1968
  SHANKS, MARGARET RICHENDA. (m James)   1940
+ SHAW, KATHLEEN A.   1940
  SHORT, HILDA E.   1980
  SHUTTLEWOOD, CECIL JAMES.   1943
    Roger Baring
  SIKES, ELSIE P.   1945
  SIMONDS, BARBARA.   1980
  SIMONDS, J DESMOND.   1980
  SINNETT, MARY.   1983
  SINNETT, RONALD.   1983
* SISMAN, JENNIFER M. (m Adrian)   1978
    Nicola
    * Jeanette
* SMART, ELIZABETH. (m Colin)   1985
  SMITH, HELEN TREGELLES. (m George)   1945
  SMITH, KENNETH MAYO. (m Violet May)   1942
    * Diane
    Alan Paul

155

QUAKERS AT SIDCOT

SMITH, MAY. 1983
SMITH, PATRICK H. 1970
SMITH, ENID JOAN. 1970
   * Daniel Felix
   * Charlotte Mii
   * Thomas Oliver
   * Gladys Omena
SOLTAU, RACHEL MARY. 1937
a SOMERS, AMY MARGARET. 1926
SOUTHERN, GRACE. 1925
   Margery
* SOUTHWELL, JOHN. 1964
+ STAINER, RACHEL. (m Duncan) 1987
   * Alice
   * Lucy
   * Sophie
STANDISH, CATHERINE M. 1929
* STEVENS, GLADYS. 1925
* STEVENSON, BARBARA. 1987
STIMSON, MARGARET. 1935
STURGE, JANE MAY. 1923
STURGE, THEODORE. 1923
   [Richard Leonard]
STURGE, RICHARD LEONARD. 1943
   * Joyce Hunt
SUNNERS, EDITH. (m Robert) 1974
+ SWARBRICK, ISABELLA LEACH. 1939
+ SWARBRICK, THOMAS. 1939
   Olaf
   Avis Margaret
   Thomas Geoffrey
   John Theodore
SWARBRICK, OLAF. (m Margaret Ann) 1952

* TANNER, DORA. (m Thomas L) 1946
   Shephen Lesley
   Virginia Lesley
TAPLIN, GRACE H. 1987
TAPLIN, PETER J. 1987
TATHAM, RACHEL M. (m Joseph N) 1951
TAYLOR, ANN. 1981
THACKERAY, MARY HOWARTH. (m Andrew David) 1945
THIEDE, PAMELA G. San Francisco 1968
THOMPSON, ISOBEL VALENTINE. 1952
THOMPSON, JOHN EDMOND. 1945

THOMPSON, JOYCE. 1945
   Richard John
   [Phillida Janet]
   [Erica]
THOMPSON, REBECCA. 1945
THOMPSON, RICHARD JOHN. (m Patricia) 1973
THREASHER, IRENE. 1983
   * David
   * Simon
TIRRELL, ALISON M. (m James J) 1975
   * Sally Elizabeth
   * Robin Jame Wallace
TOMLINSON, ARTHUR. 1960
TOMLINSON, MARGARET. 1960
   David F
TOTHILL, MABEL C. 1925
* TREGEAR, MARY. 1947
* TREGEAR, NORAH. 1930
* TREGEAR, THOMAS R. 1930
   Mary
* TREGEAR, RICHARD. 1947
TREGELLES, ARNOLD ANTHONY. 1945
TREGELLES, DAVID GOWER. 1925
TREGELLES, EVELYN MARJORIE. 1925
   David Michael
   Arnold Anthony
TREGELLES, DAVID MICHAEL. 1945
TREGELLES, HERBERT GOWER. 1928
   Hugh Gower
   Arthur Timothy
* TRINDER, ELVINA M. 1955
TRITTON, HARRIET. 1926
* TURNER, CLARA. 1943
TYLOR, P DOUGLAS. 1951

VINCENT, DOROTHY. 1964

WALLER, ETHEL. 1976
WALLER, FRANK. 1976
WALLER, THOMAS. (m Eileen) 1976
   * Nicholas
   * Antony Wright
+ WALLIS, ROSS. 1985
+ WALLIS, BARBARA. 1985
+ WARD, M JOYCE. 1950
* WARD, VICTOR. 1985
WARMAN, ELIZABETH. Bromley, Kent
+ WATERFALL, BRENDALIN. 1970

* WATTERS, CHARLES. 1989
* WATTERS, TAMARA ROSEMARY. 1989
  * Joseph Dominic
  * Shane John
  * Dominic Aubrey
WATTS, GEOFFREY H. (m Lilian)(m Renee) 1950
  [Malcolm Lehany]
  [Vincent Challacombe]
WATTS, JAMES. 1939
WATTS, JESSIE. 1939
WEST, LIONEL LINDSAY. 1942
WEST, CECILY. 1942
WESTWOOD, MARGARET. (m Colin) Salcombe 1945
WHINCOP, LILY. (m J Rowland) 1942
WHITE, CLIFFORD CHARLES. 1937
WHITE, SARAH ELIZABETH. 1935
* WHITELEGGE, MARGARET. 1943
* WHITELEY, GEORGE. 1981
WHITELEY, NANCY. 1981
WIEMS, M CATHERINE. 1951
WILLIAMS, AMY ESTELLE. (m James Frederick) 1923
WILLIAMS, FRANK H. 1974
WILLIAMS, JOAN M. 1974

+ WILLIAMS, JAMES. 1938
WILLIS, DAPHNE M. (m Peter)
* WILLS, ERIC. 1935
WILLS, HELEN IRENE. 1935
  Joan Muriel
  Allen Rendel
  Ruth Helen
  * Frances Barbara
  * John Brian
WILLS, J BRIAN. Kumasi, Gold Coast 1953
WILSON, DORIS. 1932
+ WILSON, MARY. 1927
WINTERS, PRISCILLA. 1953
WOOD, WINIFRED L. 1985
WOODHEAD, IRWIN H. 1943
* WOODHEAD, AUDREY. 1943
  * Julie Maxwell
  * Martin
* WOODHEAD, NANCY. 1978
* WRIGHT, GRACE. 1955
+ WRIGHT, GYRTH A. 1947
WRIGHT, J KATHLEEN. 1925
WYATT, MYRTLE. 1978

YEOMANS, OLIVE. 1947

BIBLIOGRAPHY and REFERENCES

Main sources used:-

The Quarterly Meeting Minutes, which are kept at the Somerset Records Office, as are the early accounts of the Sufferings.
The Monthly Meeting Minutes, which are kept at Trowbridge, but I have been allowed to borrow them a few at a time to keep in the Sidcot Safe, with the kind co-operation of Harold Fassnidge. Most of the quotations are from these sources until the Preparative Meeting Minutes take over in the 1880s. There are 12 Vols. taking us up to the 1880s, then 10 books of PM Minutes (excluding 1875-1886, which are missing) taking us up to the present day.
The Somerset QM of the Society of Friends 1688-1699 by Stephen Morland
Stephen Morland also lent me his manuscript copy of the North Somerset MM Minutes for the same period.

Other sources and references:-

A Collection of the Sufferings of the People called Quakers by Joseph Besse, Vols. 1 and 2. London 1753
Quaker Births and Burials Register, Friends House
'The British Friend' 1864 onwards.
The Journal of George Fox ed. John Nichalls
Extracts from the Minutes and Advices of the Yearly Meeting of Friends Held in London, from its First Institution, 2nd Edition. W. Phillips 1802
The Life and Travels of Samuel Bownas, pub. London 1895
The Journal of Thomas Story, pub. London 1753
The Life of Mary Dudley (1750-1823)
References in Evans and Evans, and in the *Dictionary of Quaker Biography* (DQB) to Samuel Bownas, Patience Brayton, Mary Capper, John Churchman, Mary Dudley, Ruth Follows, John Fothergill, John Griffith, Henry Hull, and Thomas Story.
DQB was helpful too in the cases of the Hipsleys, the Tanners etc.
Sewell House: Sidcot Friends Housing Society Limited 1965-80 Wilson Baker
The History of Sidcot School by Francis Knight
The Sidcot Pageant by Evelyn Roberts
Three Lectures on the Early History of the Society of Friends in Bristol and Somersetshire by William Tanner, pub. Alfred W. Bennet, London 1858
A Mendip Valley, Its Inhabitants and Surroundings, by Theodore Compton, pub. London and Swindon, 1892
The Later Periods of Quakerism, Rufus M. Jones Vol.I
Sidcot Old Scholars' Association Report — several years
The Island — Sidcot School Magazine — several years
The Quaker Studies — Nailsea, H E Dommett (unpublished)
The Story of Quakerism, by Elfrida Vipont, Bannisdale Press 1954
The Discovery of Quakerism, Harold Loukes, pub. QHS 1960 reprinted 1981
Christian Faith and Practice in the Experience of the Society of Friends, pub. London Yearly Meeting 1960
Advices and Queries, London Yearly Meeting, 1964
Portrait in Grey, by John Punshon, Quaker Home Service 1984
Bevan and Mabel Lean of Sidcot, George Hutchinson, 1981
Courage to Grow, Ruth Fawell, Quaker Home Service, 1987
Congresbury Trades, Congresbury History Group, 1988
A History of Combe House, Christine Gladwin, 1989 (unpublished)